Make It Go . . .
IN THE SNOW

People and *IDEAS*
in the History
of Snowmobiles

LARRY JORGENSEN

Modern History Press
Ann Arbor, MI

Make It Go...In The Snow: People and Ideas in the History of Snowmobiles

Copyright © 2024 by Larry Jorgensen

Published by
Modern History Press
5145 Pontiac Trail
Ann Arbor, MI 48105

www.ModernHistoryPress.com
info@ModernHistoryPress.com
Toll-free: 888-761-6268

Distributed by Ingram Group (USA, UK, EU, AU)

All rights reserved. No part of this publication may be reproduced, stored in a retrieval system, or transmitted in any form or by any means, electronic or mechanical, including photocopying, recording or otherwise, without the prior written permission of the author.

ISBN 978-1-61599-814-2 paperback
ISBN 978-1-61599-815-9 hardcover
ISBN 978-1-61599-813-5 ebook

Contact publisher for discount on bulk purchases for sales promotions, fundraising, or educational use.

Cover and interior design/layout by Vickie Swisher, Studio 20|20.

CONTENTS

INTRODUCTION   **V**
Make It Go...

CHAPTER 1   **1**
Eliason Motor Toboggan

CHAPTER 2   **9**
Propeller Wind-Power

CHAPTER 3   **21**
"Snowmobile" The Name

CHAPTER 4   **29**
Eskimobile

CHAPTER 5   **37**
The First Snowmobile Race

CHAPTER 6   **47**
A Snowmobile in His Basement

CHAPTER 7   **51**
Screw-propelled Snowmobile Motor

CHAPTER 8   **63**
The Wormobile

CHAPTER 9   **69**
Studebaker and Snowmobiles

CHAPTER 10   **75**
Farm Tractors to Snow Tractors

CHAPTER 11   **87**
Chrysler Had Some Ideas

CHAPTER 12   **97**
Small Ideas

CHAPTER 13   **111**
Snow Ideas from Honda

CHAPTER 14   **125**
IT WAS BIG and IT WAS FIRST

CHAPTER 15   **139**
Snowmobiles on Antarctica

CHAPTER 16   **153**
Trail Blazing Pioneers

CHAPTER 17   **165**
Homemade Snowmobiles

CHAPTER 18   **177**
Snowmobile Museums

ABOUT THE AUTHOR   **185**

INTRODUCTION

Make It Go...

The challenge of powered transportation in the snow has been met through the years with ideas from explorers, creative inventors and small companies, all with new ideas often unique and sometimes successful.

The name "snowmobile" was used and copyrighted in 1917, but there were snow travel ideas before that date and certainly thousands more since that date.

The winter explorers and trailblazers sought to replace their dog sleds and snowshoes as they explored difficult locations including remote locations on the north and south poles.

Early inventors of snow vehicles often worked with available parts and pieces from other old mechanical devices. A limited supply of power sources were tried, from utility two and four cycle engines to motorcycle engines, air propulsion, and even the unusual "snow biting" screw auger concept.

The snow travel ideas from some early inventors were simply designed to solve their individual winter snow problems. Other ideas came from entrepreneurs who believed others would be impressed and want to obtain what they would create. Some of their ideas evolved into companies which prospered and now can trace their roots back to that first snowmobile idea.

Make It Go In The Snow provides a look at the history of a few of the many thousands of snow travel ideas and those enthusiasts who gave them birth.

Our goal is to simply capture and record a wide variety of snowmobile ideas, without offering judgment on any individual venture.

We pay tribute to all those ideas; past, present and future. Keep watching because more snow excitement is waiting to be created.

Carl Eliason of Sayner, Wisconsin began making "motor toboggans" in 1924 and continued to be involved with their production for 31 years.

CHAPTER 1

Eliason Motor Toboggan

The Carl Eliason Motor Toboggan built in 1924 in Sayner, Wisconsin is credited as being "the first snowmobile," a title well deserved as its early design innovations ultimately influenced the creators of today's popular snowmobiles.

The motor toboggan was the first to be propelled by an endless moving track system with cleats and slide rails, a floating suspension and padded seats. It became the first mass-produced snowmobile to be sold to the general public.

2 MAKE IT GO... IN THE SNOW

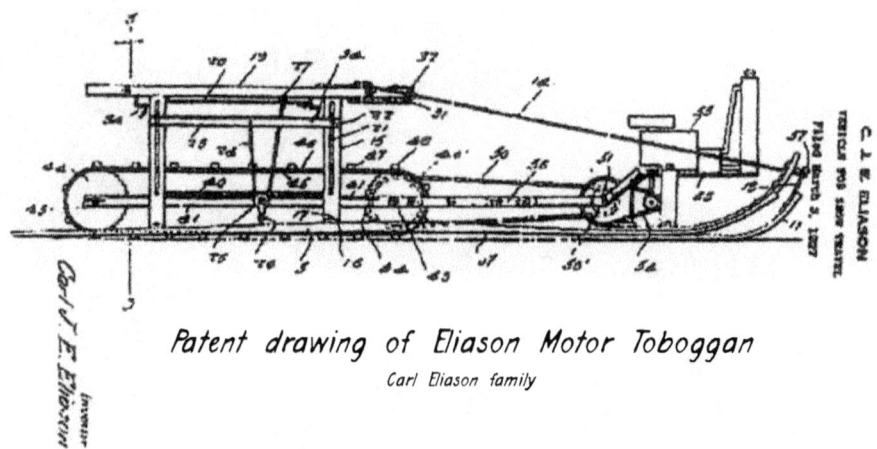

Patent drawing of Eliason Motor Toboggan
Carl Eliason family

At first Eliason had experimented with modifying a Model T Ford, but found it unworkable in Wisconsin's deep snow and unplowed roads. It took Carl two years to create the first toboggan style machine as he worked part-time in a small garage behind his general store. He patented his snowmobile designs in 1927, and to power the first toboggan he used a liquid cooled 2.5 hp Johnson outboard engine. It's interesting to note that liquid-cooled engines did not become common in modern snowmobiles until the 1970's.

Liquid-cooled toboggan engine
snowmobile.com

As he built more machines Eliason worked with a variety of two cylinder and four cylinder motorcycle engines including Indian, Excelsior and Henderson as well as Briggs & Stratton and Salisbury. These engines were preferred over Harley-Davidson due to weight and size considerations. Toboggans with two cylinder engines sold for $350, while four cylinder machines cost about $200 more.

Eventually Eliason would produce eight or nine units per year, making improvements as he worked, so few machines would be built exactly the same. The passenger capacity for the motor toboggan grew to three and four-up tandem seating.

Over thirty motor toboggans were made during those first fifteen years in Eliason's shop. The performance of the unique snow machine began attracting attention in other countries, and with the start of World War II foreign interest increased; Finland indicated a possible purchase of 200 units.

In an attempt to meet that potential demand, Carl sought production assistance from an established manufacturer. After approaching several companies he finally negotiated the sale of his patents to the Four Wheel Drive Company of Clintonville, while he would remain in a major consulting position. The Clintonville company had developed the first successful four wheel drive vehicles, and the possible toboggan purchase by Finland helped convince FWD to acquire the Eliason production. A Russian group also visited the Clintonville plant where they test drove the motor toboggans.

Production at FWD Clintonville plant

Although the anticipated purchase by Finland did not go through, an order was received from the U.S. Army for 150 Motor Toboggans to be used in Alaska. Another order was received from the Wisconsin Conservation Department for units to be used in winter patrolling. Four improved models were developed by FWD as they produced about 300 units from 1941 to 1947.

The first model produced at the Clintonville plant, the "A" model had improved steering and the 12 hp Excelsior engine was replaced with a more powerful 25 hp Indian engine.

Next the "B" model provided a foot operated throttle and had a total weight of 500 pounds.

The "C" model followed with a tiller steering handle and Indian cycle twist grip throttle. The skis were shorter and the exposed engine and track assembly were enclosed. The toboggan's total weight increased to 600 pounds.

The last Clintonville plant produced unit, model "D" was the most streamlined. It included a steering wheel with cable controlled skis. The Indian 45 engine included a three speed transmission which provided the machine with a top speed of 35 miles per hour.

After the war the demand for four wheel drive vehicles increased, while the sales of the motor toboggan had slowed. Consequently FWD decided to transfer the motor toboggan production to its Canadian subsidiary plan in Kitchener, Ontario.

The model "D" design was included in that 1947 production transfer with a goal of creating a new design for the motor toboggan which would meet the needs of the changing customer market. The first major change came in 1950 with the model K-10 which was smaller and had replaced all previous models front engine location with a new rear mounted engine.

The first rear engine design – Model K-10

Carl Eliason family

The K-10 was replaced in 1953 by the K-12 which would become the final model of the Eliason Motor Toboggan to be produced. The K-12 was promoted as an improved version of the K-10, but the two models were virtually identical with the exception of a smaller Salisbury engine replacing an 8.25 hp Briggs & Stratton and a slight design change for the rear tool box. The K-12 sold for $905 in Canadian funds and was produced for the next 10 years without any major modifications.

Motor Toboggan production at FWD's Kitchener Plant was ended in 1963 because sales during those final years had dropped significantly while the new Bombardier Ski-Doo machines were being introduced. Consequently, the FWD Corporation sold the Eliason rights and existing parts inventory to the Carter Brothers of Waterloo, Ontario. During the next year the Carter Brothers produced only 24 units before shutting down and the scrapping the remaining parts.

The pioneering design innovations and early success of the Eliason Motor Toboggan in some ways may have contributed to its own demise. As the Eliason patents expired the final K-12 model became the template for

other rear-engine snowmobile designs to follow. The Polaris Snow Traveler was first, followed by Arctic Cat, Fox Trac and others.

Several of the motor toboggan models can be seen in a small museum at the old store where it all began. Eliason hardware is operated by Carl's grandchildren John and Jona Eliason.

John and Jona Eliason at the family store museum

Eagle River, Wisconsin has become recognized as the "Snowmobile Capital of the World," and about a 20-mile trail ride away is the little town of Sayner which is honored to claim the distinction of being the "birth place" for today's modern snowmobile.

"Snow Devil." 1927 snowmobile built by Harry Jones and his brother-in-law Emil Shedell.

CHAPTER 2
Propeller Wind-Power

While Carl Eliason was working on his idea for a motor toboggan he was aware that others also were trying to create some form of a powered snow vehicle. One of those would-be inventors was Carl's brother-in-law who attempted to develop a snowmobile powered by wind from a propeller. However his project failed apparently because the weight of the vehicle made mobility difficult in deep snow. But others followed and some had success in creating wind-powered snowmobiles.

One of those successful machines was built about ten miles away from Carl Eliason's shop at a resort on Pickerel Lake. The resort was owned by Harry Jones, a pioneer resort owner in the Eagle River area, and he and his brother-in-law Emil Shedell built in 1927 a vehicle they called the "Snow Devil." It was powered by an airplane engine with a large propeller and was sleek for its time with wide skis and seating for two. A passenger and snowshoes were important to provide mechanical assistance should the engine stall. By using the snowshoes the passenger could stand on top of deep snow and hand-turn the propeller to restart the engine.

The passenger performed another important task in stopping the Snow Devil as it did not have a braking system. The passenger would jump out and attempt to hold the machine back until it stopped. Before the vehicle was built a winter time trip to Eagle River for needed supplies was a two-day snowshoe experience. The bright red Snow Devil with the words "Pickeral Lake Lodge" painted on the front made winter supply trips easier while also attracting considerable attention for the resort.

There was an even earlier successful attempt to build a propeller wind-powered snowmobile. A South Dakota newspaper, The Aberdeen Daily American, reported in 1916 how two men created a motorized "bobsled." Herman Luck and Will Stockman in Watertown, South Dakota used

Propeller Wind-Power 11

Fudge Snowplane at auction

an eight horse power motorcycle engine and an attached five foot propeller for their unusual sled. They claimed it could easily reach a speed of 30 miles per hour, but admitted that at 35 mph it became difficult to handle. The bobsled was steered by a handle and rudder-like device attached at the front.

Another old propeller wind-powered snowmobile was sold in November 2022 at a modern day farm auction in Bridgeport, Nebraska. The unique vehicle, a "Fudge Snow Plane" had been built in Canada in 1947 by Fudge Industries in Saskatchewan. When new it cost about $700.

When the auctioneer at the Kraupie Auction Company got to the Fudge snow plane the interest picked up and the seventy-five year old vehicle sold for $2,625, almost four times its original cost. The winning bidder preferred to remain anonymous so it was not known if he was a snowmobile collector or someone just curious about the unusual old machine. Whatever the reason, a 1947 Fudge snow plane had a new home.

The concept of propeller wind-powered snowmobile received considerable attention from Canadian inventors as early as the 1920's and continuing through the 1950's. Robert Fudge was one of the first to mass produce the vehicles making them available to area customers.

However it's interesting to learn that Joseph Armand Bombardier, who would later invent the popular Ski-Doo snowmobile, may also have been the first person to harness wind power for snow transportation. J. Armand was just 15-years-old when he built a wind-powered snow sleigh in his father's shop in 1922.

A year earlier his father had given him a Ford Model T engine which he believed was irreparable. However Joseph-Armand with help from his brother Leopold fixed the old engine and a year later put it to use in a snow vehicle he was designing.

He would work quietly on his project when ever he was home because he was studying at a Christian seminary, as Alfred had hoped his son would follow a family tradition and join the priesthood.

J. Armand was home on Christmas break in 1922 when finally he was able to reveal his snow machine on New Year's day. Alfred was amazed by his son's invention, but then ordered it dismantled as he was concerned about potential danger from the spinning propeller.

Bombardier's first snowmobile

Musee De L'ingeniosite, Valcourt, QC

It was about the same time in Moosomin, Saskatchewan where Robert Fudge had been working with small engines, when he decided to build a three ski snowplane using a Ford Model T engine. Three years later he started Fudge

Western Development Museum, Saskatchewan

Fudge 1949 Snowplane

Fudge Snowplane production

Industries to build what became his popular four ski models. Later he built larger snowplanes which would hold four people and reach top speeds up to 60kpm. Fudge's sales slogan was "watch the snow go by" and his snow planes sold for $600 to $800.

During the 28 years he was in business he sold over 400 snowplanes to customers including telephone and power companies, hospitals, doctors, police and individual users.

Working not far from Robert Fudge in Spy Hill, Saskatchewan was another inventor also trying to conquer the challenge of winter snow travel. Karl Lorch's first attempt in 1928 was to modify a Ford Model T by placing skis in front and chains on dual rear wheels. Not satisfied with the car's performance in soft snow he began working with the snowplane concept.

Village of Spy Hill, Sask

Lorch Snowplane

Karl built his first snowplane in 1936 using a 45 hp Ford model A engine. His snow vehicle weighed 650 pounds and sold for $850. Lorch continued production with new designs and various engine combinations. His line of models went from single person units to large snowplanes which would carry as many as four or six persons. He remained in business until 1958 selling over 600 snowplanes. Lorch was credited with being the first person to use the term "snowplane."

There were others in Canada who also built snowplanes in the 1930's, but Fudge and Lorch were the largest manufacturers. A garage owner in Minette, Manitoba Joe Davreaux built about fifteen of the snow vehicles from 1930 to 1945. Another builder in Manitoba was Fred Mansoff from Brandon who built about a dozen machines which he sold to area farmers.

By the mid 1940's Canadian roads were being better plowed and maintained reducing the demand for snow-

Lakeview Garage in Crosby where the air-sled was created

planes. In addition rural areas were beginning to outlaw the use of the snowplane claiming the horses were frightened by the engine noise.

However the idea of the snowplane was revived in the United States in 1959 when three men founded the "Trail-A-Sled" company in Crosby, Minnesota. Their original dream was to create and produce air-sleds, but their plans would change a few years later when the company became one of the nation's major snowmobile manufacturers when they created the popular line of "Scorpion" sleds.

Two other early United States snowmobile companies, Polaris and Arctic Cat also expressed interest in the snowplane idea. However Trail-A-Sled was the first to mass produce the snowplane making about thirty-five sleds from 1961 to 1963. They were powered by 90 hp Lyncoming airplane engines and could reach speeds of 100 mph. The planes held two passengers and sold for $2,590. A few four-passenger models also were produced.

Apparently Polaris saw some potential for future air-sled sales, and company official David Johnson contracted with Trail-A-Sled in 1963 to manufacturer twenty-five of the two-person Polaris "branded" air-sleds. Not to be outdone Edgar Hatteen at Arctic Cat had his own prototype air-sled designed and built.

Air-sled advertising by Polaris

Polaris sold only a few of their snowplanes before an incident caused concern that the vehicles could be dangerous and impractical. The remaining Polaris machines were said to be scrapped and buried in a landfill.

Trail-A-Sled air-sled

Scott Gottschalk Snowmobile Museum, Kimball MN

Edgar Hetteen drives reproduction Arctic Cat air sled

Arctic Cat had even less success with their brief venture into air-sleds. Their one prototype machine was powered by a 16 hp Onan engine, and an Arctic Cat employee reported after a few test runs that the sled was under-powered and performed poorly. Hetteen dropped the idea of an air-sled and no additional units were made.

Originally believed to be the next "big thing" in snow travel, the actual air-sled production in the United States had a short history of about three years in the early 1960's. However a few of those rare snowmobiles remain, mostly on display and occasionally in use.

Propeller Wind-Power 19

Dick Harrison of Trail-A-Sled with the four-passenger model and the two-passenger which he fabricated for Polaris

In Kimball, Minnesota Scott Gottshalk's museum of over 300 old and unique snowmobiles includes three air-sleds. One is a rare four-place Trail-A-Sled plane, another is a Polaris model and the third is a reproduction of the Arctic Cat which was made to scale and includes the actual skis used on the original prototype.

Other locations where air-sleds can be viewed are the "Miracle of America" museum in Polsom, Montana and the Volo Museum in Volo, Illinois. Another sled was offered for sale by an apparent collector in 2015. Identification on the sled's side indicated it may have been used by the U.S. Coast Guard as an experimental vehicle.

Air-sled at museum in Montana

Air-sled offered for sale in 2015

CHAPTER 3

"Snowmobile" The Name

What is a snowmobile? In the current unabridged Random House dictionary, a snowmobile is simply defined as "a motor vehicle with a revolving tread in the rear and steerable skis in the front for traveling over snow."

That might be a modern day definition, however, the name "snowmobile" actually was copyrighted in 1917 by a Ford dealer who claimed he created the name "snowmobile" after he designed and built a snow travel attachment for a Ford Model T. Virgil White built that first attachment in 1913 at his auto business in Ossipee, New Hampshire, and he received a patent for his invention in 1917. With White's attachment the rear wheels were replaced by dual heavy-duty wheels covered by tracks with metal cleats. A pair of large wooden skis on metal frames were attached to the car's front spindles.

White boasted that his attachment made it possible for the Ford to travel 18-miles-per-hour over two and a half feet of snow. He formed a business in 1919 which he called "The Snowmobile Company" where he built and sold Model T Fords with his patented invention. The price for a completed Model T was $750.

Snowmobile Company advertising (above) and manufacturing plant (below)

White then spent several years perfecting his idea to create an attachment kit. Henry Ford was impressed with the invention and the kit was placed on the market in the winter of 1922 being sold exclusively by Ford dealers. The kit sold in New Hampshire for $395.

That first winter about 70 of the new kits were produced and sales grew quickly during the following years. In 1923, to meet the increasing demand, Wright sold the rights to also manufacture and sell the kits to the Farm Specialty Manufacturing Company in New Holsten, Wisconsin which then began producing its own version of the kit which they called the "Snow Flyer."

The following year the Wisconsin company purchased all of White's patents as well as his "Snowmobile Company." They sent managers to run the plant in New Hampshire and changed the company name to the "Snow Flyer Corporation." About 3300 kits were being manufactured each year and also were being made available for other cars including Chevrolet and Whippet.

Advertising on Snowmobile Company Ford

"Snow Flyer" snowmobile

The New Hampshire plant was closed in 1929 and less than a year later a fire of unexplained origin totally destroyed the building along with all remaining plant records and drawings.

However the Snow Flyer Corporation in Wisconsin continued to make the kits available, and another company in New Holsten also began producing a snow vehicle attachment. The ARPS Corporation founded by Bruno Arps in 1926 made and sold a kit called the "Snow Bird." It was made available for both Model T and early V8 Fords.

A 1929 Model T Tudor Sedan with an ARPS conversion was purchased by the New York Guard. The Snow Bird received national recognition in 1931 when it was used on Admiral Byrd's second antarctic expedition. ARPS named the vehicles "Super-Snowbirds" as they promoted their expedition use in company advertising.

SUPER
Snow Bird
Six Wheeled
For
MODEL AA
TRUCKS

Hyman Ltd

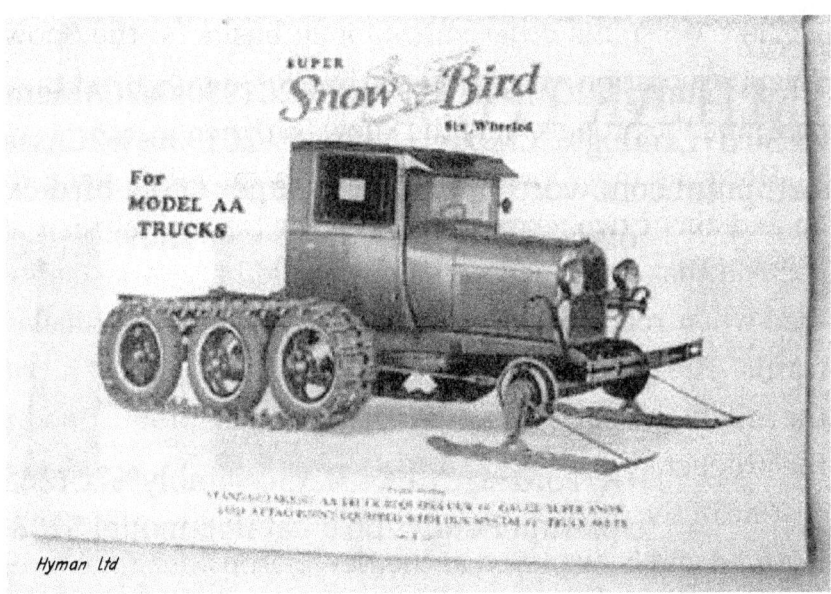

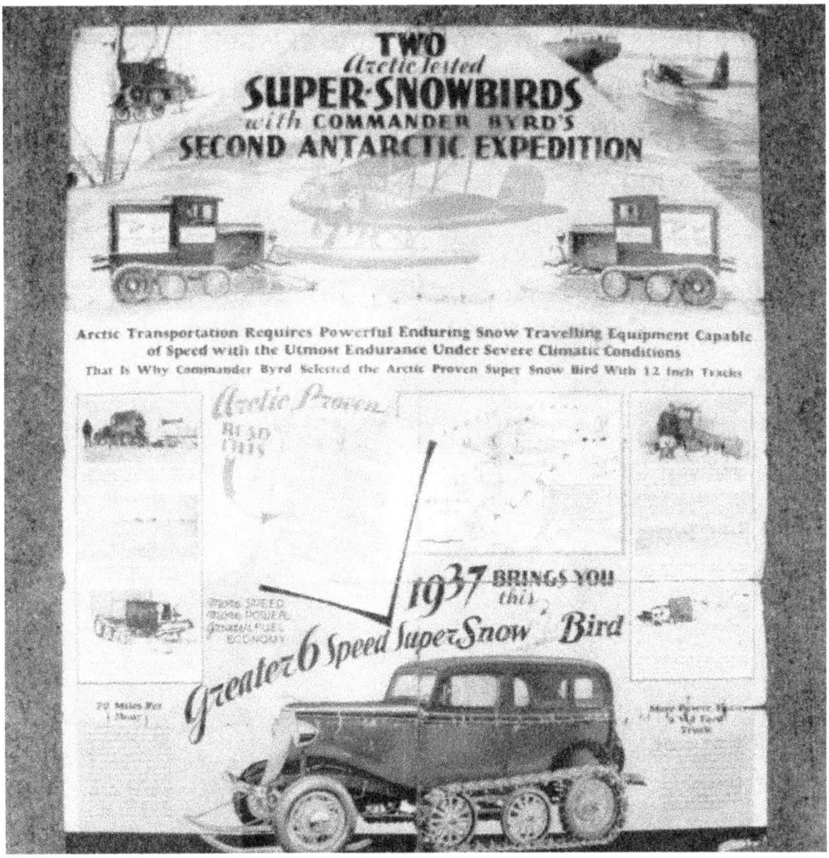
TWO
Arctic Tested
SUPER-SNOWBIRDS
with COMMANDER BYRD'S
SECOND ANTARCTIC EXPEDITION
Arctic Transportation Requires Powerful Enduring Snow Travelling Equipment Capable of Speed with the Utmost Endurance Under Severe Climatic Conditions
That Is Why Commander Byrd Selected the Arctic Proven Super Snow Bird With 12 Inch Tracks
Arctic Proven
1937 BRINGS YOU
this
Greater 6 Speed Super Snow Bird

New Holsten's other snowmobile business, the Snow Flyer Corporation was purchased by ARPS in 1933, but they continued to produce only the Snow Bird kits.

However the snowmobile business for ARPS came to an end about two years later when the U.S. Postal Service decreed that rural mail no longer would have to be delivered when roads became impassable to regular vehicular traffic. The government decision eliminated almost all of the Snow Bird sales and ARPS discontinued production of the product.

One of the original 1925 Model T snowmobiles has been restored and is displayed at the New Hampshire Snowmobile Museum in Allentown. The car had been dismantled and the parts were in poor condition when it was donated to the museum in 1989. Volunteers and donations made possible the difficult restoration which finally was completed in 2009.

Original Model T Ford snowmobile

New Hampshire Snowmobile Museum

Model T Ford Snowmobile Club

Another restored Ford snowmobile is on display at the "Midwest Dream Car Collection" in Manhattan, Kansas.

It's believed at least 400 of the Ford snowmobile kits are still in existence and one home for the rare vehicles is the "Model T Ford Snowmobile Club" which was formed in 2000 to preserve the history and use of the Ford snowmobiles. The club has over 200 members, including some in other countries, and at least seventy members are owners of Model T snowmobiles. Many of them display their rare snow vehicles at club events held each year at various snow country locations.

It was discovered that a non-snow use was possible with the vehicle when the skis were replaced by wheels; the old Model T became useful in deep and heavy sand. Nicknamed a "sandmobile" it was reported to have been used in the Florida everglades and in foreign locations like South Africa and Egypt.

Preserved snowmobile

This 1923 Ford snowmobile was originally sold by Ford dealer George Chesley in Dover, NH. It is believed to be the best preserved original Model T snowmobile. The paint, top and interior are considered original and untouched, and the skis and metal tracks are the ones sold with it.

CHAPTER 4

Eskimobile

While the ARPS Corporation was busy making "Snow Bird" snowmobiles in New Holsten, another Wisconsin company over 200 miles away had developed their own ideas for producing snowmobiles. The Eskimobile was one of three snow vehicles manufactured and sold by the Swansen Machine Company of Almena, Wisconsin.

Brothers John and Henry Swansen started the company in 1920 to manufacture farm equipment. The brothers were the perfect team for their new business as John was the "idea man" and Henry was the innovator whose mechanical talent in the shop would create the products from John's ideas.

John had seen a photo of a snowmobile attachment on a Ford Model T and asked Henry to build something similar in their shop. What evolved in the early 20's was the Eskimobile, an improved snow attachment which became available in different design options. A company sales brochure proclaimed the attachment "had been perfected by eight years of extensive development." It was first available in two different sizes at a cost of $250 when purchased at the Almena plant.

The attachment was designed with a modified suspension allowing the tracks and skis to be unbolted providing year round use of the vehicle. An advertisement for the Eskimobile called it an "all year car adaptable to your needs assuring comfortable transportation for all seasons and under all road conditions."

Swansen Machine built at least 180 Eskimobiles between the years of 1921 and 1941. Eskimobile customers had three purchase options.

Henry Swansen takes a lunch break after delivering fuel oil for Standard Oil.

They could simply buy the attachment and self-install it. They could bring their car and have the attachment installed or they could purchase an entire car complete with the attachment. The complete cars were created from Model T and Model A Fords, and at least one used a Dodge. Eventually Swansen would purchase the car chassis and bodies to create their cars.

When purchasing a complete car the customer was provided with an option to obtain his vehicle piecemeal by purchasing the chassis and body in spring for warm weather use and then adding the winter attachment in the fall. The completed Eskimobile car sold for $850, and for an additional $20 John would personally deliver the car and demonstrate its use.

There would be an occasional time when a customer could not immediately pay the total cost of his snow vehicle. For those situations the buyer was offered the op-

portunity to work off the remaining amount in the shop by doing anything from welding to sweeping the floor.

A special feature of a Swansen built car was the built-in sliding doors, replacing the regular doors which opened outward. It was said the sliding doors provided improved ventilation for warm weather and storm-tight closure for cool or rainy weather. The Eskimobiles used a "Ruckstell Axel" which provided four speeds forward and two in reverse.

A sales brochure boasted that "Eskimobiles were in service in almost all snow-covered states as well as Alaska and Canada." It was reported that Eskimobile races were held for several years in Alaska. The brochure added that the snowmobile was produced to "fully meet the rigid requirements of rural mail carriers, doctors, dairymen, farmers and others."

The innovators at the Swansen Machine Company also produced two other vehicles to deal with the challenge of snow travel. One called a "Stiltmobile" was an early elevated vehicle designed to travel the rural roads frequently covered with melting snow and heavy mud.

The Stiltmobile which sold for $750, had greatly enlarged tractor type front wheels and large truck tires on the

rear. It had a specially designed body which included elevated fenders.

The "Sno-Tank" was the third vehicle made by the Eskimobile manufacturer. The tank was designed for traveling across deep snow-covered fields, swamps and marshes, and through heavy brush. It had longer tracks and runners and operated similar to a Caterpillar tractor. The tank had eight speeds forward and could travel up to 40 mph.

The Sno-Tanks were available in two sizes. A small tank would carry two people and was powered by a single engine. The larger tank was powered by two engines and could carry ten passengers.

From October to April the crew at Swansen Machine Company worked on Eskimobiles, Stilts and Sno-Tanks. The rest of the year they produced farm equipment. World War II forced the company to close in 1942 as it lost most of its work force and business and was confronted with the added difficulty of obtaining supplies needed to continue manufacturing. Available steel was needed for the war industry and auto manufacturing also had been shut down.

Swansen Machine Company was a rural small town manufacturer which had innovative ideas to "make it go in the snow."

Original or restored Eskimobiles are rare and difficult to locate. Unlike other better known antique snowmobiles there is no organized group of users and the task of preserving the Eskimobile relies on individual collectors. One of those collectors is Tony Rolfes who maintains his snowmobile collection and other vintage vehicles at his business near Brainerd, Minnesota.

Eskimobile 35

Eskimobile in like-new condition discovered in Upper Michigan

The snowmobile portion of his collection is focused on antique sleds built before 1966. Consequently an opportunity in 2005 to obtain an original condition Eskimobile piqued Tony's interest. The sled was located at a cabin near Ironwood, Michigan and the owner contacted the collector explaining that a tree had fallen on his "track type" snowmobile and he wanted to sell it not knowing it was an Eskimobile.

A trip to the cabin by Rolfes confirmed the vehicle's actual manufacturer was Swansen Machine, a deal was made and the Eskimobile found a new home in Tony's collection. The fallen tree had damaged the snowmobile's roof, but that turned out to be the only repair work needed.

The like-new condition of the Eskimobile always attracts attention and questions when displayed at vintage snowmobile events.

Another old Eskimobile, but in worse condition, was purchased by Rolfes at an auction in Brook Park, Minnesota. The snowmobile was turned over to Henry Swansen's grandson David Matthys who was restoring it along with help from two cousins. David is known as the family historian as he and his wife have compiled scrapbooks and maintained accurate records of products produced by Swansen Machine Company. The historic photos in this chapter were provided by David Matthys.

CHAPTER 5
The First Snowmobile Race

When and where was the first snowmobile race held? It's been suggested that the first snowmobile race "probably was held when the second snowmobile was made."

However 1964 in Eagle River, Wisconsin is often considered to be the date and place for the first organized sled competition. Other events and places have challenged that claim, but the Eagle River race continued to grow and has become recognized by many as the oldest and largest snowmobile competition in the United States.

It all began as an idea by resort owner John Alward who was seeking a way to attract more winter visitors to the area. He and his wife Betty organized and promoted that first event which was a cross country type race held on Dollar Lake near their Chanticleer Inn. The race started and ended on the lake and included a steep hill climb and trail with a sharp turn.

Dollar Lake race site

Alward family photo

The First Snowmobile Race 39

Alward family photo

The first Eagle River winner

World Championship Snowmobile Derby Archive

Stan Hayes receives his first race trophy

It was hoped that a dozen or more snowmobile owners would compete before a gathering of a few hundred spectators. However advance promotion of the unique new event attracted over 100 competitors and an unexpected crowd of several thousand. The inaugural race winner was a 13-year-old student Stan Hayes from Crandon, Wisconsin. Later snowmobile racing became an important part of Stan's life as he achieved national fame as a driver on the Polaris professional factory race team. For his first victory in Eagle River he drove a 9 hp Polaris.

The following year the race again was held on Dollar Lake and attracted even more racers and a much larger crowd of spectators making it apparent the event had outgrown the limited space available at the lake location. The race was turned over to the local Lions Club which relocated the entire event to a prepared oval course in town and they trademarked the race as the "World Championship Derby." With a new location, name and sponsor the derby flourished to annually attract drivers from several countries and crowds of over 50,000 fans for two weeks of competition. The race has been referred to as the "Indianapolis 500 of snowmobile racing."

However with all the success and international attention to Eagle River, the site for the first snowmobile race remains challenged. In fact, two other northern Wisconsin communities not far from Eagle River also have claimed to be sites for those first races. One of those is Rhinelander, about 25 miles southwest of Eagle River where a new snowmobile dealer believed a race in 1961 would get some attention and maybe a few buyers for his new Ski-Doos. It was just a few months earlier when boat dealer Fred Gates had received his first shipment of three new machines to become one of earliest snowmobile dealers in the country.

Fred discovered the first buyers were hard to find as it seemed people had little faith in those new mechanical sleds. However, after finally selling a few he reasoned that a competition among his first buyers might attract new customers. An ice fishing jamboree had been scheduled for January on nearby Boom Lake and Gates was allowed to hold his race event at the jamboree.

Five new Ski-Doo owners showed up at the starting line along with about a thousand curious spectators to witness this new winter event. Fred waved his arm and the race got underway taking the riders on a round trip course around an island about a half-mile away. The winner had just purchased a new nine horsepower snowmobile, the most powerful model available, and he cruised to an easy 15-length victory at an estimated speed of 30 miles per hour.

Next Fred solved a last minute problem of a trophy for the winner by giving him an unopened bottle of brandy he had left in his truck. The winner, 60 year old Herman Lassig shared his trophy with fellow racers.

After the race Fred admitted more needed to be done to improve the credibility of the snowmobile. Because the race had been held on an ice surface many still doubted the potential for traveling through deep snow in the woods.

Rhinelander's first snowmobile racers: Lionel Bellile, Ron Strum, Herman Lassig, Mike Taylor, Alex Sharka. The winner Lassig is in the center.

Another claim for the first snowmobile race comes from a different type of race which was held twenty-five years before the Rhinelander event at a small community about 10 miles south of Eagle River.

It was January 31, 1926 in Three Lakes, Wisconsin when two Ford Model T snowmobiles faced off on a frozen lake about a mile north of town. Ironically the race turned out to be another competition of sorts between Eagle River and Three Lakes as there was an entry from each community. The Eagle River car, driven by Harold Hanson, had been prepared by the Strong and Manly Ford agency in that city. Bill Neu of Three Lakes drove a Model T snowmobile prepared by the Badger Garage of Three Lakes.

The snowmobile race was the featured attraction in the city's first winter sports carnival and attracted over 200 people to the race site. In their attempt to win, the Eagle River Ford crew had overhauled the engine, but apparently failed to break it in sufficiently and the engine was too tight. During the race Hanson's car overheated and he was forced out before the end.

Three Lakes Museum archives

Snowmobiles getting ready for the first race

Neu's Ford apparently was better prepared as it had a special carburetor and overhead valve. Neu drove to an easy win and received a .22 caliber rifle as his winner's prize.

North of the border Canada has its own "bragging rights" for the first and best known snowmobile race. The annual Canadian Power Toboggan Championship began in 1963 in Beausejour, Manitoba. But it actually was a snowmobile event a year earlier which provided the idea for the Power Toboggan race. Six drivers had participated in a competition in 1962 at a wine festival also held in Beausejour.

An even earlier event took place in 1958 in The Pas, Manitoba when a planned snowmobile demonstration at a festival became an impromptu competition. The demonstration of six Polaris Sno-Travelers became a race when the drivers decided to add some excitement to the event by

Spectators crowd the finish line at an early race in New York

competing at speeds up to 20 mph on the oval track.

Snowmobiles were providing an interesting new concept for winter travel and recreation in the 1960's and people were anxious to learn more about them. The idea of racing to create more interest and excitement quickly spread throughout snow country.

The state of New York was one of the first eastern states to attract the early races. One of them was in 1963 at the Malone Winter Carnival. The Saranac Lake Carnival also conducted a race in 1963, and in 1965 a race at Madrid Springs attracted 75 competitors.

Additional New York race sites in the mid 1960's included Booneville, Lake Placid, Warrensboro, Tupper Lake, Pottersville, and others.

Saint Paul, Minnesota was the location for a different type of snowmobile competition in 1964 when 40 racers ran along the lakeshore at Phalen Park.

And a snowmobile dealer in Marquette, Michigan had the idea of using racing to promote his new business. Bud Wessen was a Ski-Doo dealer and he decided in 1962 to invite 15 customers who had bought sleds to participate in a race in a field near town. To add to the excitement grudge races were held between the Marquette police chief and the county sheriff, and between the mayors of Marquette and Escanaba.

When Wessen held the race again in 1963 he added 3-foot high bumps to the track and "Sno-Cross" competition was born.

The final answer to the when and where question about the first snowmobile race may never be truly established.

But what is certain it all began because someone had an idea and some of those ideas, like Eagle River and Beausejour have grown to become iconic traditions in modern day snowmobile competition.

CHAPTER 6
A Snowmobile in His Basement

The 1926 Model T Ford snowmobile race in Three Lakes was not the first time snowmobile history was made in that northern Wisconsin community. It was 1911 when a summer visitor had an idea to build a snowmobile which he could use for planned future winter visits to the area.

Model R Ford

Ray Kuhl probably conceived his idea during a summer visit with his sister Viola Leatzow and her husband Charles at their lakeside cottage. After his visit, Ray returned to his home in Chicago and decided to build a snowmobile in his basement. He was 15 years old and already had acquired mechanical experience by working on early model Fords;

The Ford Model R used by Ray to build his snowmobile

Ray Kuhl and a Chicago neighbor Leo DuMaisgive give Ray's homemade snowmobile its first test run

knowledge which became valuable for his snowmobile project.

Using just basic hand tools and parts from a 1906 Model R Ford, it took Ray only a month to construct his unusual boxy-looking snowmobile. To provide the power for his creation, he connected the Ford engine to a drive chain which then was connected to a large farm wagon wheel which had been positioned at the rear of the elongated snow vehicle. Bolts were added to the wheel's rim to provide traction, and the wheel was firmly bolted in place causing it to bite into the snow. The radiator from the Ford was positioned at the front to provide maximum engine cooling. Four skis for the unusual sled were made of two-inch wide wood, covered with four-inch wide sheet metal allowing the snowmobile to slide over the snow.

When Kuhl finally hauled his machine from its basement birthplace, he was able to travel over limited Chicago snow cover at a speed up to fifteen miles per hour. He explained deeper snow would provide better traction and make it possible for his new snowmobile to travel even faster.

Later, Ray found the improved snow conditions he was seeking in Three Lakes, and he and his wife Edna eventually became full-time residents when they purchased a home on Spirit Lake.

Ray Kuhl died in 1971 at the age of 81. However, before his death, he was able to admire the performance of modern-day snowmobiles when he attended the 1968 Eagle River Championship Snowmobile Derby.

GPI — Gorsky PolyTechnic Institute

CHAPTER 7

Screw-propelled Snowmobile Motor

A screw-propelled snowmobile is based on an idea and design principle created by Archimedes, a Greek mathematician who lived between 287-212 BC.

When put into modern day use a snowmobile is moved by auger-like grooved cylinders. The rotating cylinders bite into the snow to pull the vehicle forward.

Peavey Locomotive Snow with snow motor

The first screw-propelled snow machine was patented in 1907 by Ira Peavey of Maine for use in the lumber industry. It was called the "Locomotive Snow" and was powered by an internal combustion engine and had snow motor attachments on each side. It was designed to haul logs but because of its length and rigid construction it had difficulty traveling on the uneven rough winter roads.

Next to utilize the screw-propelled design was the Armstead Snow Motor which was developed in Michigan in the early 1920's. The Armstead device was mounted to a Fordson tractor and was being built in the Ford factory. An early successful use in Oregon was by a stage line which cleared the road over Mackenzie pass between Eugene and Bend, Oregon. The Hudson Bay Company ordered machines to help provide contact with northern fur trading stations,

Armstead Snow Motor

and the Canadian Royal Mounted Police also purchased the snow machines.

In addition auto companies including Chevrolet, Dodge and Hudson considered the possibility of adapting the snow motor to their cars, and interest also was being received from Norway, Sweden and Alaska.

An Armstead promotional film actually showed the snow motor fitted to a Chevrolet, and it also demonstrated a Fordson tractor unit which was pulling a 20-ton load of logs.

The increasing interest in the Armstead Snow Motor also attracted the attention of a group of Detroit auto maker who in 1925 formed a company called "Snow Motors Inc." to purchase the snow motor and further promote the development and sale of snow motor vehicles. A. F. Knoblock

Fordson pulling logs, L'Anse, MI

was listed as the corporation's president and general manager. Henry Ford also was active in the new company and a promotional film showed Ford at the wheel of a Fordson snow tractor demonstrating the vehicle's performance in Michigan's wet snow.

Ford had purchased a lumber mill near L'Anse, Michigan on Lake Superior in 1922. The mill was surrounded by 30,000 acres of hardwood forest and daily produced up to 180,000 board feet of lumber which was shipped 80 miles south to Ford's factory in Iron Mountain. A photo of the Fordson snow tractor pulling a sled load of wood was taken in 1926 in the L'Anse area. The Snow Motors company stated the snow machine was specially adaptable to lumber operations in northern communities.

Plans for an expedition which could bring international fame for the Fordson snow tractor began to fall in place on May 27, 1925 at the annual meeting of the Detroit Aviation Society. Ford announced at that meeting the recent completion of factory experiments which proved the snow tractor was capable of hauling heavy loads of logs, building roads and other heavy hauling demands in the "north country where transportation has long been a serious problem."

The timing of the announcement was important as the Aviation Society and the National Geographic Society were planning to sponsor the 1926 Detroit Arctic Expedition and the Fordson snow tractors could provide a much needed role in the Alaskan adventure. The purpose of the expedition was to provide aerial surveillance of previously unexplored areas of the polar sea to discover new lands and if possible occupy them for the United States.

The planes to be used for the exploration were to be flown to Point Barrow, and three Fordson snow tractors would lead a caravan of ten sleds carrying 15-tons of airplane fuel, radio equipment and other supplies for the waiting aircraft. The snow tractor caravan was critical to the mission's success because expedition plans had been made too late to provide sufficient time for shipping the fuel and supplies to the base camp at Point Barrow.

Three snow tractors were shipped to Nenana, north of Fairbanks to be assembled at the place where their 1000 mile journey would start on February 10, 1926. Prior to their scheduled departure the Alaska Road Commission conducted two short trial runs with a snow tractor, and after the tests declared in their opinion the tractors "would not be able to cope with the Arctic conditions." The local sled dog mushers also did not believe their teams could be replaced by "mechanical Malamutes."

However the local population became enthused about the snow tractor's ability to complete their planned mission after a public demonstration was held January 25th in Seward, Alaska. The event concluded with the snow tractors being christened at a formal ceremony. The tractors and their ten giant sleds then were loaded on the Alaska railroad for the trip back to Nenana and the start of their adventure.

The expedition quickly encountered unexpected problems as they traveled on honeycombed ice which was covered by 15-inches of sand-like snow resulting in traction problems for the rotating snow motors. In addition the sub-zero temperatures were causing castings and other parts to fail with the supply of spare parts becoming exhausted.

Fordson Snow Tractor being tested in Alaska

Caravan fails

In twelve days the caravan had traveled only 65 miles and already used over 400 gallons of gasoline. In an attempt to improve their travel the caravan was broken into four sections with one tractor taking two sleds to go ahead and break the trail. Another tractor then would relay remaining sleds three at a time. After more time consuming delays the snow motor sled train idea was abandoned at Tolovana, and alternate means of getting fuel delivered were considered. A caravan representative radioed ahead explaining that even if the snow tractors made it to Point Barrow there would not be gasoline left for the planes as it would all be burned up by the tractors.

Air transportation for the fuel was ruled out as the closest possible landing site on a frozen river was a risk. In addition the planes would be required to limit their loads so they could fly over the 9,000 foot high Brooks mountain range.

Finally sled dog teams were pressed into service and after 63 extremely difficult days they delivered enough fuel to permit a very few of the planned flights. Good flying time at Point Barrow can be limited to two months, and often visibility was so low that flying was impracticable and the expedition accomplished little.

After the failed expedition one team member when questioned by the press said "we didn't accomplish much but we enjoyed the experience."

What happened to the abandoned snow tractors remains a mystery. But one ended up being possessed by a Fairbanks resident and later it was acquired by the Pioneer Air Museum to be displayed for several years. Next it was loaned to the Fountainhead Antique Auto Museum in

Restored Arctic Expedition Snow Tractor
Fountainhead Antique Auto Museum Fairbanks

Fairbanks where it was restored to operating condition. It remains on display along with a demonstration film of the unique snowmobile which is said to be the only operational Fordson Snow Tractor in the world.

Michigan state records indicate the company known as "Snow Motors, Inc" which had been organized in 1925, was dissolved a short time after the failed Arctic exposition. However new ideas continued for the use of the screw-propelled snow motor concept.

One idea in 2002 was another Arctic challenge which came from two British adventurers who planned to build a specialized snow vehicle to cross the Bering straits ice bridge from Alaska to Russia. Steven Brooks and Graham Stratford selected a Bombardier snow groomer and added the Armstead screw propulsion system. Called the "Snow Bird 6" it had to float on water, drive through solid and crushed ice and climb onto icebergs while operating in temperatures as cold as -40 below.

"Snow Bird 6" another arctic adventure

Maritime Journal

The 56-mile straits would freeze for just a few weeks each year, long enough to even make the trip feasible. It had never been done before and it would be a difficult part of the total expedition from New York to London for what was to be the longest-ever overland trip.

The team and their snow machine waited several days in Alaska until the weather cleared and when they decided to leave they still had not received final clearance from Russian authorities, but hoped they would get the approval while enroute. However after 12 hours into the trip Russia advised they could not land and would be arrested if they did.

The explorers then decided to change course and headed to the International Date Line, the official border with Russia. The "Snow Bird 6" was left on Little Diomede Island just east of the date line inside U.S. territory and about halfway across the straight. Six years and $750,000 had been spent on the failed attempt.

The screw propelled snow motors for the Snow Bird had been made in Russia, and it was later revealed that the motors would not have been strong enough to complete the planned mission. After the Snow Bird was abandoned one of the snow motors was found floating in the ocean and was retrieved by a barge crew from Prudhoe Bay.

Ideas to put it back into service were ended after closer inspection and the snow motor was abandoned north of Fairbanks at the town of Wiseman.

Screw-propelled Snowmobile Motor

Les Zehicles Tout-Terrain

Russian inventors had been working with the concept of screw propelled snow motors for decades. The Motorbob Sleigh built in 1927 was one of the earliest.

GPI — Gorsky PolyTechnic Institute

In the 1970's an attempt to use them on modern snowmobiles apparently was made by the Gorky Polytechnic Institute in Gorky, Russia.

GPI — Gorsky PolyTechnic Institute

Screw propelled snow motors also were used for some Russian military units and for rescue vehicles which could retrieve returning cosmonauts from remote locations such as Siberia.

In the United States they have been some homemade backyard projects to create screw propelled vehicles...

...and in the 1920's one was put to test when dozens of curious spectators crammed on board a sled being towed by a snow motor car.

CHAPTER 8
The Wormobile

The concept of a screw-propelled snowmobile was reactivated in 1952 as a joint project involving seven machine and engineering companies in the Sheboygan, Wisconsin area.

It appears the lead company for the idea may have been Feldman Engineering because a review of the company's history shows a continued interest in snowmobile and all terrain vehicles. Feldman created the Terra Tiger ATV in 1969, and then built and sold the Sno-Flake mini-snowmobile in 1971. The parts for the Sno-Flake may have been

Sno-Flake snowmobile

excess inventory from the Couparral Company in Minneapolis acquired by Feldman after Couparral quit making the line of Sno-Pony sleds. The Sno-Flake and the Sno-Pony had a common appearance and performance.

Other companies who participated in the Wormobile project included Holden Machinery a Sheboygan manufacturer of parts, and Langjars Blacksmith Shop in Plymouth. It required over two years to complete the project with at least five other companies involved in welding and providing components.

The Wormobile was built on the chassis of a 1940's Willys Jeep. It was powered by a 4-cylinder Jeep engine and one of its three transmissions was also from a Jeep. The other two transmissions came from Model A Fords, and were used to control the screw drive attachments.

A variety of other vehicle parts were also included in the final product, including a Dodge truck hood and headlight, a grill from an Allis-Chalmers tractor, an international seat and an Oliver #70 gas tank and radiator. When completed the Wormobile was 7.5 feet long and 6.5 feet wide.

The intended end use for the machine was not revealed, although some speculated it might have been planned for winter mail delivery in rural areas of Wisconsin. However the unusual snowmobile turned out to be too slow and difficult to handle. Finally it was left abandoned for about thirty-five years in a wooded area in Shawano County, west of Green Bay.

It was in that location when the old snow vehicle was discovered by Harold Erdman, a retired machinist from Manitowoc. Erdman said it was in rough shape, but that

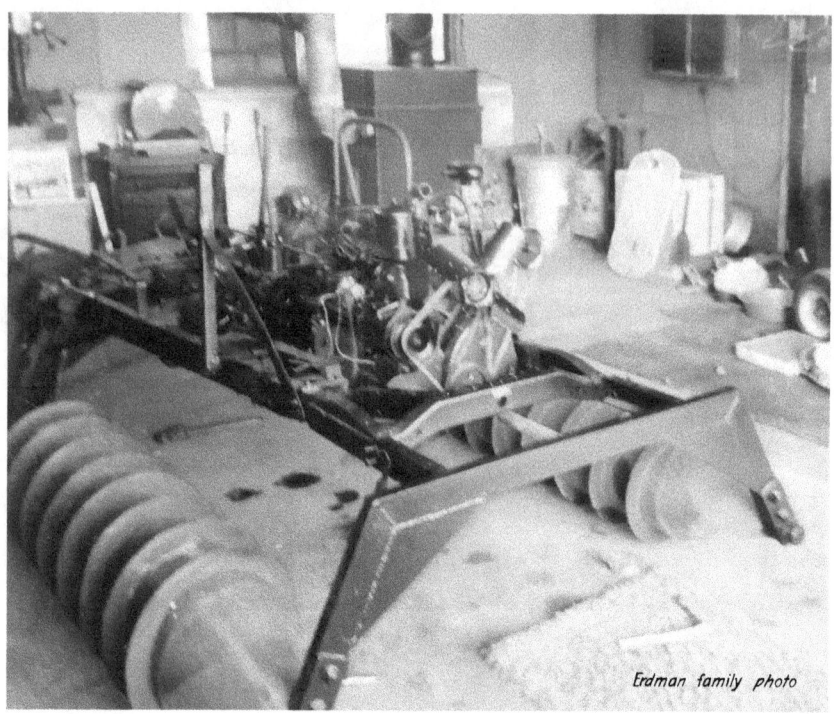

Erdman family photo

didn't stop him from acquiring the machine because he said he had plans for it. Previously Erdman had restored several old tractors, and he was a member of a vintage vehicle organization.

Harold said there was no doubt the Wormobile was one-of-a-kind and would be the most unusual machine he had ever restored. The work was done in the garage at his home in Manitowoc where the snow vehicle was torn down to its Jeep chassis.

After several months of dedicated work and some assistance from an interested neighbor, the restoration was completed and ready for display. Harold took the machine to steam engine shows and other vintage vehicle events where it attracted considerable attention and many questions.

Erdman family photo

Harold said he often would be asked what the Wormobile was used for and he'd reply "I really don't know." In addition he explained the machine "traveled rapidly sideways but not very fast forward or backward."

Harold Erdman died in 2020 at the age of 90, but his restored oddity continues to attract curious spectators at shows and at a museum. It was purchased by a vintage snowmobile and vehicle collector, Tony Rolfes of Rufus Ranch in Brainerd, Minnesota. Tony then drove vehicle a few times and displayed it at shows throughout Minnesota. Lacking adequate space to properly store his Wormobile, Tony finally placed it on display in 2023 at the Top of The Lake Snowmobile Museum in Upper Michigan.

Harold Erdman with his restored Wormobile
Manitowoc Herald Times Reporter

Minnesota Historical Society Collections

CHAPTER 9
Studebaker and Snowmobiles

It was January 1922 when the "Go Devil" a homemade ice boat was revealed to a photographer from the Minneapolis Morning Tribune. Even though it was not built by the Studebaker Car Company the unusual machine had a close connection to Studebaker.

It had been built by O.H. Gray and Wilbur Hammond. Gray was a well known Minneapolis Studebaker dealer operating "Gray Motor Company" located in the "Studebaker Building" on Hennipen Avenue.

Shortly after that initial press demonstration on Lake Calhoun this second photo was professionally taken and the Studebaker identification had been added to the side of the sled.

Minnesota Historical Society Collections

During the first demonstration Gray informed the press he planned to display his snow creation a month later in the Minneapolis Auto Show as part of his Studebaker exhibit area. The Studebaker logo apparently had been added for that show and any future promotions. The photographer's notes on the back of the photo indicated it was to be used in a Sunday newspaper advertisement.

Gray's unique sled was said to be capable of speeds up to 100 mph. It was 18-feet long, weighed 1400 pounds and was powered by a 125 hp airplane engine. Those smaller size airplane engines had only recently been developed by automotive engineers in Detroit.

Gray was a well known dealer for the Studebaker Company, and in 1916 had been included on a committee of five dealers who selected a prominent previous customer to receive a one-week expenses paid trip to a major auto show.

It was twenty years later when the Studebaker Company actually got into the production of a snow vehicle. The U.S. military realized in 1942 the need for a new type of transportation to be used in WWII. To be called the "Weasel" it would have to move quickly and easily through snow. It would carry troops with explosives, arms and equipment.

The Studebaker Weasel
Collection of Studebaker National Museum, South Bend, IN

The Weasel also had to be able to be transported by plane and withstand the effects of being dropped by parachute.

Early design consideration was given to the idea of the Weasel being powered by a screw-propelled Armstead type snow motor. That idea was strongly supported by British inventor Geoffrey Pike who had been involved in the earlier Fordson Snow-Tractor Arctic expedition. Pike had received some interest from the Canadian military, but after that failed the idea was then presented to the American military, and Pike moved to the U.S. to oversee development of his plan.

However fellow planners said Pike was very inflexible with his idea and finally lost support of others in the project development. Ultimately a conventional track type Weasel was approved, and Studebaker was selected to build them.

Studebaker Weasel production line

Studebaker and Snowmobiles 73

Studebaker war time advertisement

A total of 15,890 Weasels were built for the military for use during the war. The Marines used the Weasel for one of its first appearances in combat at Iwo Jima in 1944. It was used by the Army during the Battle of the Bulge and numerous other operations. They also were used by the

British Special Service Brigade and by the British infantry divisions. Both amphibious and non-amphibious Weasels were made, and after the war many Weasels were kept in service for several years.

An exhibit featuring the Weasel during the war can be seen at the Studebaker National Museum in South Bend, Indiana.

CHAPTER 10

Farm Tractors to Snow Tractors

Allis-Chalmers was another American company which manufactured a snow vehicle for the military. The huge Wisconsin company was a pioneer of the industrial age, making engines and machines used around the world. But they may be best remembered for their line of bright orange painted farm tractors.

M7 Allis-Chalmers Snow Tractor

The company started producing machinery for agriculture in 1914 and grew to become a world leader in that industry. In 1944 they manufactured the M7 Allis-Chalmers Snow Tractor for the U.S. Army Air Corps. The Air Corps 10th Mountain Division used the Snow Tractor with an attached sled to rescue downed pilots and to haul needed materials.

The men of the 10th Mountain Division fought during World War II in Italy's northern Apennine Mountains, some of that country's roughest terrain. The Allis-Chalmers snow machine helped the Air Corps improve mountain rescue tactics. The elite soldiers of the division had trained at Camp Hale in the Colorado Rocky Mountains.

Farm Tractors to Snow Tractors

The Snow Tractor weighed 2610 pounds and was powered by a Willys Jeep powertrain. The use of Jeep components lessened the military's spare parts inventory needs. The machine ran on two large rubber belts and skis could replace the tires. The skis were made of wood with a metal sheath underneath. A canvas cover would be fitted over the tractor for cold weather protection. The unit had a top speed of 41 mph.

During the development of the Snow Tractor, prototypes had been created by Emmett Tucker, who later became famous for his Tucker Sno-Cat machines.

Camp Hale
Colorado Rocky
Mountains

The Snow Trailer pulled by the tractor was manufactured by the Saginaw Products Company which started in 1919 in Saginaw, Michigan as a tool and die company. In 1927 they were purchased by the Chevrolet Motor Division which owned the business when the trailers were made for Allis-Chalmers.

The trailer weighed 640 lbs and could carry a payload up to one ton. It also had a canvas cover along with removable side frames. When used for rescue two stretchers and a personnel heater were positioned under the canvas. The sides could be removed when the trailer was used for hauling cargo.

About 300 Snow Tractors were produced by Allis-Chalmers, and one of them has been restored and is on display at the Roberts Armory World War II museum in

The Snow Trailer was manufactured by the Saginaw Products Company which started in 1919 in Saginaw, MI

A restored Snow Tractor is on display at the Roberts Armory World War II Museum in Rochelle, Illinois

Rochelle, Illinois. After the war many of the tractors were put to a new use when they were owned by farmers in western snow mountain areas.

The Snow Tractor on display in Illinois was in poor condition when located in Idaho by museum owner Chuck Roberts. He and his wife restored the unit by making a new canvas top, fixing the track, and making new skis and some side panels.

The museum displays artifacts from the war with a special emphasis on the 10th Mountain Division. The museum is open only for a very limited number of days during the year, but arrangements to visit can be made by calling 815-561-4445 or email to ccr@robertsarmory.com.

Allis-Chalmers introduced a new six wheel amphibious recreational vehicle called the Terra Tiger; a vehicle "for all seasons and all terrain."

About twenty years after creating the snow tractor Allis-Chalmers decided to explore the potential of the new recreational vehicle market. The 1960's had become a financially challenging time for the company with plants being closed and business relationships changing.

Allis-Chalmers leaders apparently took note of the then flourishing ATV market as a means to generate new income. The company introduced a new six wheel amphibious recreational vehicle called the Terra Tiger, available in two versions, a lower priced 10 hp model and an 18 hp unit complete with electric start and a greater top speed. They called it a vehicle "for all seasons and all terrain."

However Allis-Chalmers did not develop their Terra Tiger in house. It had been created by Marvin Feldman of

Feldman Engineering in Sheboygan Falls, Wisconsin, and it was credited as being one of the leading amphibious ATV designs of its era. Feldman sold the Terra Tiger rights to Allis-Chalmers but would continue to manufacture the vehicle at his plant. Feldman's prototype models were painted with a red and white design but Allis-Chalmers had the color changed to a dark lime green.

Terra Tiger assembly line

The Terra Tiger weighed 600 lbs, was powered by JLO single cylinder two-stroke engines and had a top speed of 30 mph on land and about 4 mph in water. It was manufactured from 1969 to 1971 and Allis-Chalmers was able to establish a small dealer network while promoting the Terra Tiger with colorful brochures, advertising in targeted consumer publications, and displays at outdoor expositions.

Terra Tiger promotional brochure

However the demand for a six wheel amphibious ATV dropped quickly with the introduction of the three wheel and ultimately the quad bikes.

Allis-Chalmers also considered manufacturing their own snowmobile, and proof of that brief attempt is the one remaining prototype of three actually produced at the company's plant in suburban Milwaukee. That rare snowmobile is on display at the Top of the Lake Snowmobile Museum in Upper Michigan, and how it got there is a story which begins with a determined Allis-Chalmers employee.

The company, best remembered for its popular orange painted farm tractors, decided in 1965 there would be a need for a utility work-type sled instead of a recreational use snowmobile. They might have considered the utility machine would be a better fit for their well-established farm equipment market.

However it appears the company was not fully committed to the idea with only three prototype models to be built and then only during the plant's production "down time," and by using as much as possible existing assembly line components. For example, the snowmobile hood was made from tractor fenders and a piece from an Allis-Chalmers combine. The seat was gray vinyl similar to a tractor seat.

Two of the prototypes were identical and powered by 4-cycle Lloyd OHV engines with four speed and reverse transmissions and electric start. A smaller 2-cycle engine was tried on the third sled but it proved to be under powered, as the machines each weighed over a thousand pounds.

After additional testing of the prototypes, Allis-Chalmers decided the snowmobile idea was not practical and all three were placed in a disposal scrap area. However a company shift foreman Roy Stewart and another employee each secretly salvaged one of the 4-cycle sleds and took them to Upper Michigan. Stewart brought his machine to his father's farm near Iron River, while the other one went to the Calumet area in the Copper country where it was used only for a short time before problems caused it to be junked.

Stewart's sled was used on the farm for several years until a broken spindle created a steering problem and it then was stored in a barn for over thirty years.

Ownership of the snowmobile ultimately was transferred to Doug and Darla Bonno of Iron River after Doug had discovered the sled while working in that area. Doug

84 MAKE IT GO... IN THE SNOW

Allis-Chalmers snowmobile prototype

became concerned the rare sled would be destroyed and thought it needed to be in a museum. The owners agreed it should be displayed and with that commitment they decided to sell it to the Bonnos for the scrap value of $100.

Doug did some restoration work and the one surviving Allis-Chalmers snowmobile was placed on loan at the Upper Michigan museum.

At one time the Allis-Chalmers company had over 30,000 employees and was a world leader in industrial manufacturing. However by the 1980's and 1990's the company had sold off its major business components and the divestitures transformed the company causing it to eventually be dissolved and shut down its remaining Milwaukee area facility in January 1999.

Chrysler Defense Engineering

CHAPTER 11
Chrysler Had Some Ideas

Chrysler also considered building a vehicle for war time use. It was in the 1960's for the war in Vietnam and a power concept which had been used before for snowmobiles was included in Chrysler's design plans. Although there would be no snow in Southeast Asia, screw propelled power became the choice for the proposed new military transportation craft. The vehicle had to be capable of operating in marshy areas and in areas inaccessible by boats such as the Mekong Delta region of South Vietnam. Both the Navy and Army had reported a need for this type of vehicle.

Chrysler was a major player in military transportation having built 25,000 Sherman and Pershing tanks for World War II. The military selected Chrysler in 1963 to build the first of two vehicles for Viet Nam and both would use the counter-rotating screws. The initial machine called the "Marsh Screw Amphibian" weighed over 2,000 pounds and was powered by a 225 cu. inch slant-six cylinder engine. It could carry a half-ton payload of six fully equipped combat troops.

The Chrysler all terrain vehicle also had been designed to operate in snow, but because the military's immediate need was for use in Viet Nam the new vehicles were tested only in the south, and their possible performance in snow was never determined.

The Marsh Screw machine was sent for testing to the Army Corps of Engineers Research and Development Center in Vicksburg, Mississippi. The testing engineers

The Marsh Screw machine

The Chrysler Riverine

reported the machine performed well in free water but "failed miserably" on soil surfaces especially sand, where it became immobilized because of inadequate power. It also experienced trouble crossing obstacles such as simulated rice-field dykes and the steering mechanism was described as poor. In addition the flat side design allowed the screw motor to toss mud into the unit.

Despite the disappointing results for the "Marsh Screw" craft, Chrysler was selected in 1969 to produce for the Navy a much larger vehicle called the "Riverine Utility Craft." This second unit which had a payload capacity of one ton could carry seven combat ready soldiers and a crew of two. Chrysler produced ten of the Riverine units and again one of them was tested at the research facility in Mississippi. The actual testing sites included areas in south Louisiana where conditions resembled those of the Mekong Delta.

The Riverine craft exhibited greater water speed and unique capability of performance in highly restrictive areas not accessible by other craft. However no additional Riverine units were made after the military decided to continue using more conventional vehicles.

For a brief time Chrysler then promoted the marsh craft as a "swamp buggy" for recreational use and for hunters. One of each of the prototype units remains on display at the Corps of Engineers Research Facility in Vicksburg.

A Chrysler "swamp buggy" on display

Chrysler directed its attention in 1975 to the increasing popularity of snowmobiling with the idea of creating something new for that market. The result was called "Sno-Runner," a single person sled which they produced from 1979 to 1982. Possibly described as a "moped-type" vehicle, it had a single ski in front for steering and a

The Chrysler Sno-Runner

68-inch long rubber track powered by an eight horsepower engine built by West Bend, a Wisconsin company Chrysler had purchased in 1960. The Sno-Runner had a single speed gearbox with a centrifugal clutch. It had a twist grip throttle, hand lever brake, headlight and taillight, and a kill switch next to the throttle.

It weighed about 71 pounds and was collapsible to easily fit in the trunk of a car. It could barely reach a top speed of 40 mph and proved to only be capable of travel on groomed snow and flat terrain. The Sno-Runner sold for $700, quite a bit cheaper than a full size snowmobile, but some considered it expensive because of the limited use problems.

The idea for the Sno-Runner had been presented to Chrysler by Steven Quick, an engineer who was then hired by Chrysler and became the project manager for the development and production of his idea. At that time (the

The Chrysler Sno-Runner military version

pre-Iococca years) Chrysler was experiencing desperate financial problems and it was thought that becoming involved in the booming snowmobile business would improve the company's bottom line.

Chrysler also believed that once again there could be potential sales to the military which was looking for a snow vehicle that could be broken down to fit into a sack, air dropped and easily re-assembled in the field. However the Sno-Runner never made it beyond preliminary testing with the military. Chrysler also viewed ski resorts as another prospect for Sno-Runner sales, but due to the vehicle's low power performance that idea also produced few results.

Chrysler promoted the Sno-Runner to potential customers with full page advertisements, colorful brochures and videos. However after two years only 30,000 of the small snow vehicles had been produced and Chrysler halted production in 1982. The unsold inventory was liquidated by a company called COMB which sold the units for $299.

Chrysler Sno-Runner full page advertisement

The Sears XS22 Sno Bike

But the Sno-Runner idea apparently didn't die when Chrysler stopped production. It may have inspired others to take a look at the concept of a "snow cycle" type of snowmobile. One of them was Sears which developed their product with the Roeper Corporation in Bradley, Illinois and called it the Sears XS22 Sno Bike. It shared patents for the track system with the Chrysler Sno-Runner. The Sno Bike was an even smaller vehicle and it is believed only six of them were made before testing showed it to be unacceptably dangerous: Sears shut the program down.

However Sears did make other efforts to sell snowmobiles to its customers. In 1965 an agreement was made with the Trail-A-Sled company to provide units for Sears, and it was also reported that Polaris provided a limited number of Sears snowmobiles.

Another single person snowmobile called the "Skee-Whee" was designed for year round use. It was sold by FS Industries of Evanston, Illinois and had two skis in front which could be replaced by flotation tires for all seasons use.

The Skee-Whee

The Clinton All Terrain Bike

One other different approach to the idea of small snowmobiles came from a company known for its small engine and mini-bike production. The Clinton Machine Company produced what they called the "Clinton All Terrain Bike," which also was track powered but had a mini-bike appearance for the front tire design. The Clinton Company was located in Maquoketa, Iowa where it produced over 18 million engines to become a world leader in small engine manufacturing.

The Yardman Sno-Cub

CHAPTER 12

Small Ideas

The early 1970's were innovative times in the development of the modern day snowmobile as new ideas were being developed, tested and presented to potential customers. Some companies, like Chrysler experimented with the single person cycle-type snow vehicle, and there were even those who developed snow transportation adapter kits for existing motorcycles. However there were others who believed mini-snowmobiles might be a better idea, and two companies, one in Michigan and another in Minnesota, were among the first to produce the small sleds which, for a few years attracted interest and buyers.

The Yardman Sno-Cub was a mini-snowmobile manufactured by the Yardman Company in Jackson, Michigan. The Sno-Cub weighed only 125 lbs, had a 10-inch track and was powered by a 4.7 hp 99cc JLO engine. The model years listed for the Sno-Cub were 1970-1972. However one was seen as early as 1969 in Wisconsin communities where it was being used in summer parades to help promote the state's first snowmobile show to be held that September in Green Bay.

The Yardman Company was started in 1933 to manufacture outdoor tools and tractors, being best known for its original silent Yardman hand powered lawn mower. Yardman products were primarily sold at Montgomery Ward department stores, and Yardman also produced a small sled for them called the "Mini 99." The Montgomery Ward version was identical to the Sno-Cub except it was painted orange instead of yellow and it had special decorative trim.

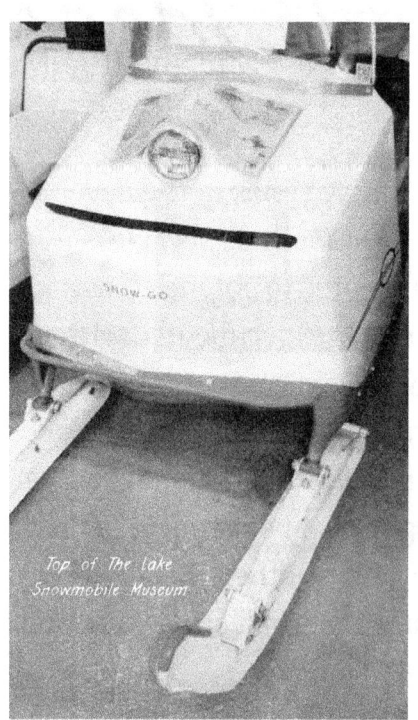

Riverside Snowmobile

The Yardman produced sled was not the first snowmobile sold by Montgomery Ward. In 1966 Polaris produced the "Riverside" standard size snowmobile for Wards, which was said to basically be a Polaris Mustang with a different red and white color design.

The Riverside Caribou

In 1967 Montgomery Ward sold the "Riverside Snow-Go" and in 1968 the stores sold an improved model called the "Riverside Caribou." It's believed the Caribou was made in Sweden. Wards introduced another sled in 1977 called simply the 450, a 30 hp snowmobile apparently manufactured by Gilson Brothers of Plymouth, Wisconsin.

Wards 450

Ky Michaelson

The idea of a small snowmobile became more interesting after a colorful Minnesota inventor and entrepreneur Tony Fox created the Sno-Pony in his Bloomington garage in the early 1960's. He also established the Couparral Corporation in 1967 to manufacture his line of Sno-Ponys which he called "the new generation of snowmobiles." The designer and test engineer at Couparral from 1968 to 1972 was Ky Michaelson who later became nationally known as "The Rocketman" because of his speed achievements in the world of fast machines.

Couparral manufactured a line of five Sno-Pony snowmobiles which weighed 170 to 200 pounds and were 75 to 81 inches long, depending upon the model selected. They had a 15-inch track and bogey system and four types of engines were used; the 180 and 220 Solo and the 295 and 340 JLO. Sno-Ponys sold for $649 and $699 and were promoted as an economical alternative to a standard snowmobile.

Sno-Pony models

Sno-Pony brochure

Sno-Pony twin engines

Sno-Pony became involved in snowmobile racing in 1969 and 1970 when a special race model was produced which had been developed by Ky Michaelson. The sled had an unique power system that linked a pair of McCulloch engines which were being successfully used in go-cart racing. Each engine size was 101cc, which gave the race sled a total engine size of 202cc's. The U.S. Snowmobile Association (USSA) stock A race class specified engine sizes of 250cc's or less. The Sno-Pony racer sold for $1,000 and it was a winner at its first race, a USSA sanctioned event in Brainerd, Minnesota.

The Sno-Pony had been raced in the Stock-A class of competition but their victory was protested by some who claimed the Sno-Pony was a modified sled not a stock model. The protesters referred to USSA rules which required at least one-hundred models of a specific sled to be manufactured before it could be considered as stock. With

Sno-Pony racing

that issue under discussion Tony Fox provided a document which indicated 103 of the Sno-Pony racers had been produced. From there the twin engine Sno-Pony went on to

Sno-Pony winners

win or place in many future Stock-A races.

Next Michaelson had an idea which could gain national recognition for Sno-Pony. It would be an attempt to establish a new world's land speed record for snowmobiles, and he knew that the vehicle to set that record was a jet powered drag car which was located in Milwaukee and might be for sale. The car had been designed in part at the Illinois Institute of Technology in Chicago and was being built by Pete Farnsworth and fellow enthusiasts in Farnsworth's Milwaukee garage under the business name of Reaction Dynamics. However Farnsworth was forced to halt work on the jet car due to other business and family demands.

Michaelson revealed to Tony Fox the information about the jet car and his ideas on how to use the car to establish the snowmobile speed record. Fox became convinced of the potential for the project and the two of them went to Milwaukee and successfully purchased the "Sonic Challenger XI" from Farnsworth.

Michaelson collection

XI Rocket

To prepare for the snowmobile land speed record attempt, Michaelson's changes included replacing the car's wheels with 56-foot skis on the front and rear. The record run was held February 14, 1970 on Lake Champlain in Burlington, Vermont. The event was sanctioned by the United States Snowmobile Association and witnessed by a representative of the Guinness Book of World's Records, which at that time had listed the record speed at 96.33 mph.

XI Rocket conversion

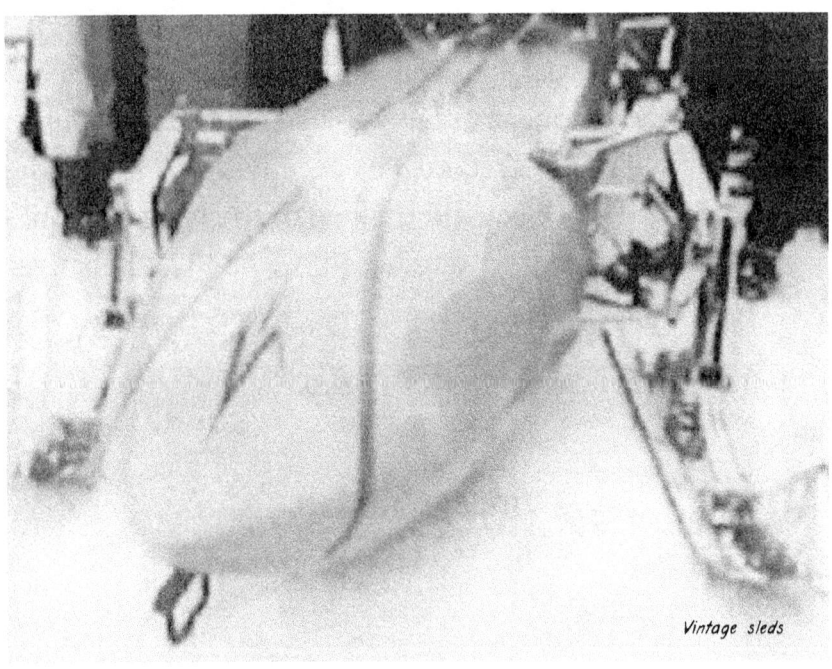

Vintage sleds

Sno-Pony archives

Michaelson collection

A crowd watches the speed run as a new record is made

Over 1500 fans had gathered in sub-zero temperatures at the frozen lake site to watch the speed challenge which had been scheduled for 9:30 am. However the run was delayed until afternoon to allow time for the runway to be scraped after Michaelson surveyed the surface and complained it was not smooth. When everything was right the Sonic Challenger made the run in just five seconds, setting a new world's record of 114.5 miles per hour. A half-mile run off area and a custom built chute were required to stop the 1,000 pound sled. The chute was ripped in the process which prevented Michaelson from making a second run at the record.

After setting the record Michaelson said "I wish I could have done better." He explained the high speed caused the front of his snowmobile to lift and affect his ability to steer and stay on the course. He said he was forced to keep the speed at half throttle and claimed the 3,000 horsepower jet was capable of reaching speeds up to 300 mph.

After the run it was initially feared the USSA would not recognize the new speed record because the association rules required the snowmobile to operate with a track, and the Sonic Challenger had only skis. However USSA race director Dick Clark after reviewing the rules explained there was a special classification for experimental snow vehicles and the new record became official.

Michaelson collection

Michaelson after the speed run

Tony Fox (standing) and Michaelson inside the Challenger

That record setting run also must have been a bitter-sweet achievement for rocket sled owner Tony Fox because that same year he had sold his Sno-Pony interest to a company called Sports Power, Inc. of Saint Paul. The Couparral Company continued to produce the line of Sno-Pony snowmobiles and the Sonic Challenger was used in company advertising and in displays at shows and other snow related events.

The new Sports Power company was owned by the Gravely Division of the Studebaker-Worthington Corporation of South Bend, Indiana. A Studebaker representative said Sports Power planned to build other products including a possible larger size snowmobile. Michaelson built a prototype of the larger sled but it was never produced. Michaelson also had designed an optional wheel kit which gave the Sno-Pony additional use in non-snow conditions.

Financial problems plagued Studebaker in the 1960's forcing the company to produce its last automobile in 1966. Production of Sno-Pony snowmobiles was halted in 1971 with the remaining sleds and parts along with the Sonic Challenger moved to a Studebaker warehouse in South Bend for storage and liquidation. The Newman & Altman Standard Surplus business sold the remaining Sno-Ponys for $298 each, and replacement parts were reported as difficult to find.

Ky Michaelson went to South Bend and was able to purchase the engine for the Sonic Challenger from Studebaker. The remaining rocket sled was painted red which covered all logos and identification, and was sold to the owner of

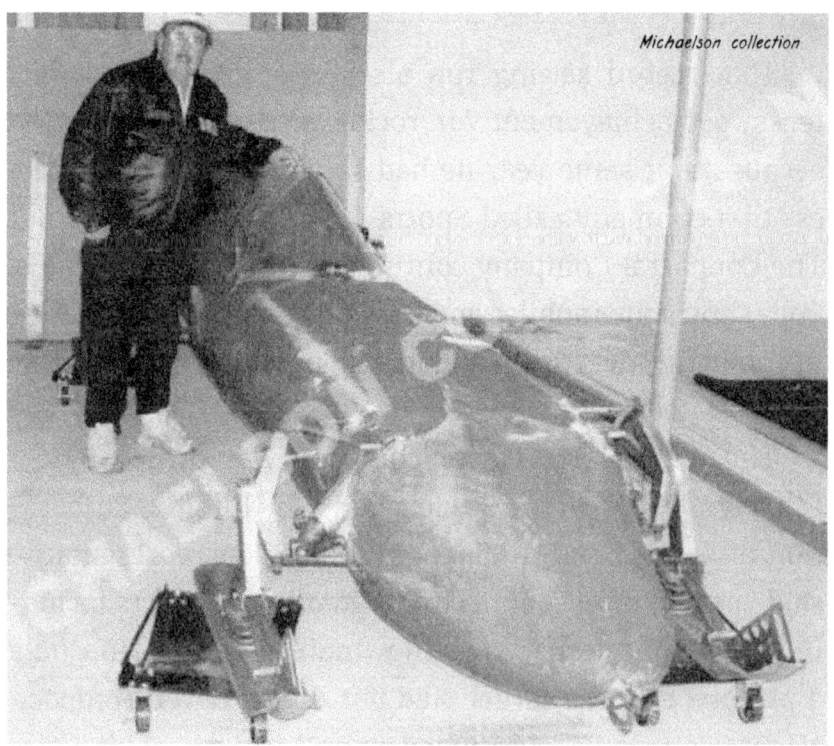

Michaelson with red painted Challenger in South Bend

Rocket sled on parts store roof

Blue Flame establishes world record

a snowmobile parts business in Niles, Michigan. The drag sled then became a promotional attraction when it was placed on the roof of the snowmobile parts business which later also became a motorcycle shop.

Several years later the original builder of the Challenger, Pete Farnsworth had the ability and still the desire to pursue his original dream of building the first hydrogen peroxide rocket dragster. He located the car, re-purchased it and took it back to Milwaukee to begin creating what would become the world famous Blue Flame rocket car.

On October 23, 1970 the Blue Flame driven by Gary Gabelich on the Bonneville Salt Flats established the world land speed record of 622.407 miles per hour. The record remained for over fifty years and was officially commemorated in the states of Wisconsin, Illinois and Utah.

Ford Ice speed record

Detroit Public Library

The Sno-Pony Sonic Challenger's record speed run on frozen Lake Champlain in 1970 helped draw more interest to what had become the new modern day type of snowmobile. However it wasn't the first speed record to be established on a frozen lake.

It was sixty-six years earlier when another new vehicle set a world's record on Michigan's frozen Lake St. Claire. Located northeast of Detroit between Michigan and Ontario, Canada the lake's frozen smooth surface became a popular site winter for auto testing and speed runs.

It was Henry Ford along with his driver Ed Huff who in the winter of 1904 used a new Ford to set a one-mile speed record of 91.37 mph. The ice surface had been conditioned with hot cinders to improve traction, and the event which had been publicized in advance, attracted viewers in autos and on ice boats.

Ford returned to Lake St. Claire again in 1912 with a specially built race car and his factory driver Frank Kulich who was able to successfully handle the racer for another new record of 109 mph.

automotorpad

CHAPTER 13
Snow Ideas from Honda

Honda cycle dealers throughout the snow country by 1970 were letting it be known they needed a Honda snowmobile to be able to compete with other dealers in the new and rapidly growing snowmobile business.

Hearing that call to action, Honda announced to their dealers that a snowmobile would be coming soon because an agreement had been made to work with a well known U.S. snowmobile manufacturer. It turned out that this would be the first of several ideas and prototypes to be developed by Honda during the following years.

A prototype of the Honda snowmobile

The first Honda sled was an experiment with Polaris Industries and used a chassis manufactured by Polaris. Dealers got their first look at what was being developed during dealer meetings in the spring of 1971 where they learned their new sled would be powered by a 750cc Honda 4-stroke motorcycle engine.

An actual prototype of the Honda snowmobile was unveiled in February of 1973 at a meeting of dealers in Marquette, Michigan where the reaction was described as cool. The dealers had anticipated their Honda snowmobile would be a departure from existing lines of sleds, but most also believed it would be powered by the industry standard 2-stroke engine.

The concern by dealers was that the four cycle motorcycle engine and gearbox would make the sled too heavy, and also that it would need to sell for around $1800, making it among the most expensive models in the 1974 season.

The White Fox single person snowmobile

Unable to gain sufficient dealer support for the 4-stroke concept, Honda turned to their snowmobile development program reportedly based in Greendale, Wisconsin. Instead of another large snowmobile, Honda went to the opposite extreme and created a 227-pound machine powered by a 10 hp 178cc 2-stroke engine. Called the "White Fox" the single person snowmobile was designed for youngsters or adults weighing up to 150 pounds.

The engine was mounted in the rear with a torque converter drive system and a 14.6 inch track which consisted of twin tracks mounted closely together. The White Fox was 79-inches long and 32-inches wide with the driver sitting with legs extended forward. Honda boasted the highly engineered sled had been tested at high altitude in the South American Andes and had a top speed of about 40 mph.

The White Fox was officially announced to dealers by American Honda Motor Company in a Christmas eve letter dated December 24, 1973. The letter called the new machine "revolutionary in every sense of the word," saying it was a pilot project which would be carefully studied and evaluated.

The first and only production run of the "White Fox"

The initial and only production run of the White Fox consisted of about 300 units with 200 of them being made available to selected dealers only in Wisconsin and Michigan. Then less than five months later Honda made a surprise announcement that they would not produce or market the White Fox and all existing inventory was being recalled.

No official reason for the recall decision was given, but what appeared to be a hasty announcement caused considerable speculation. There was a rumor of a serious accident and some believed there was the potential for litigation because of the legs-forward design of the White Fox. Others surmised the decision was made because of the gas crisis and its related slowing of sales in the snowmobile market.

One report said the recalled sleds were crushed and buried in a Wisconsin landfill. Another story said the snowmobiles were taken to Japan to be crushed. However at least five of the White Fox snowmobiles escaped the crusher. One which is on display at the Top Of The Lake Snowmobile Museum in Naubinway, Michigan is owned by Joe Jones of Boyne City, Michigan. Jones sells NOS parts for motorcycle brands and had acquired his White Fox from a cycle dealer.

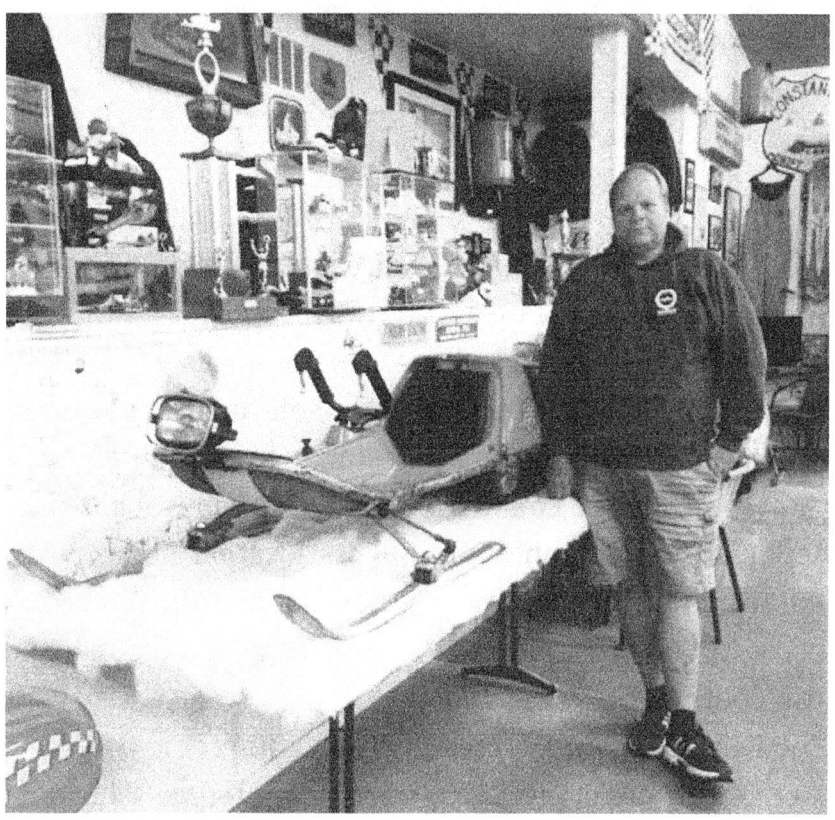

Joe Jones with his White Fox at the Top of the Lake Snowmobile Museum

Snow Fox on display in showroom

Two more White Fox sleds were purchased from a snowmobile broker by the owners of Northeast Vintage Cycle in Springville, New York, and one remains on display on their showroom floor. The other one was sold and last it was reported to be on display in a museum in the Netherlands.

A fourth White Fox was obtained by a snowmobile museum in Washington state, but its location became unknown after the museum was closed. The fifth Honda reportedly was painted to cover its identification marks and was sold at an estate auction.

While Honda was creating the White Fox they also were exploring other ideas to create prototype sleds, and they established a relationship with the Leisure Vehicles company in Troy, Michigan which was manufacturing the

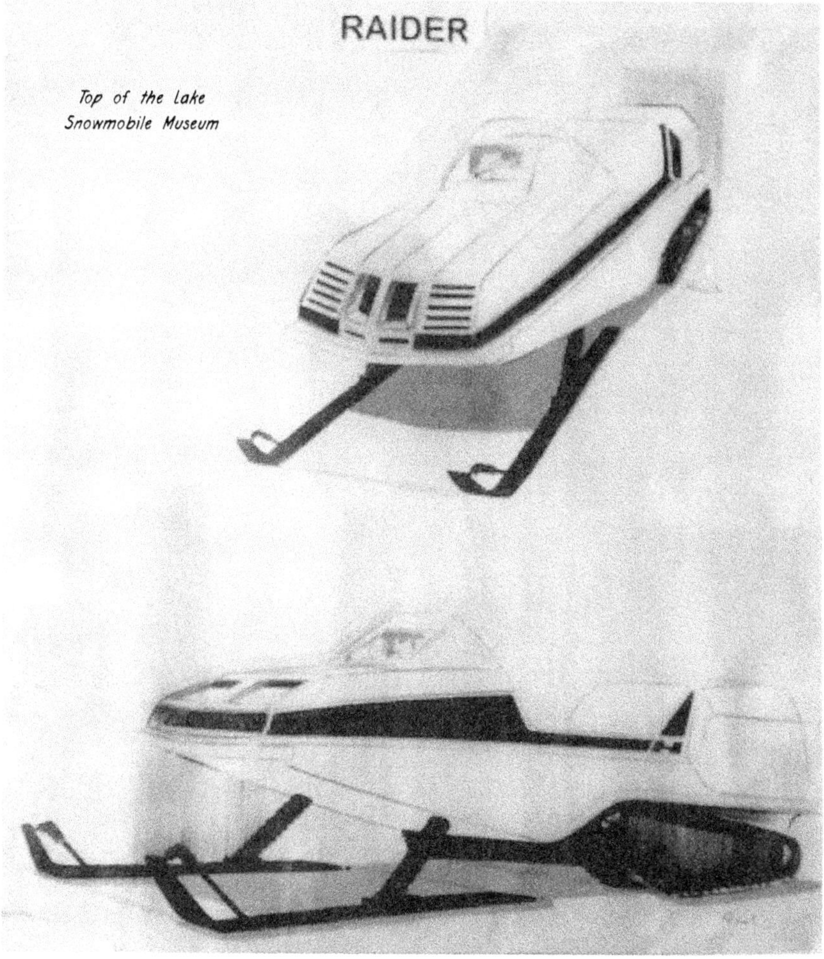

Snow Ideas from Honda

RAIDER

Top of the Lake Snowmobile Museum

The Raider Snowmobile by Leisure Vehicles company

Raider Snowmobile. The company had been started by Bob Bracey an automotive engineer who had worked for each of Detroit's big three auto makers, and then became a pioneering entrepreneur in snowmobiling. The Raider had a new sit-in design instead of the

Alain Benoit and Gregg Dobberke at snowmobile museum

standard sit-on sled, and it was one of the first twin track style snowmobiles.

In 1972 Bracey created a prototype Raider 44TT which Honda would use to test some new ideas. Included in one sled was a CCW (Canadian Curtiss Wright) engine and a Salisbury hydro transmission. Two other test Raiders also were built for Honda and each was fitted with a Honda Engine. One of the two Honda powered sleds is believed to still exist and was reported to be owned by a collector in the United States.

Leisure Vehicles company Raider-style prototype

The one CCW Raider is owned by Gregg Dobberke of Oshkosh, and it is on display at the Top of the Lake Snowmobile Museum in Naubinway, Michigan. Dobberke's Raider was originally sold at auction when the Leisure Vehicles Company went out of business. After being allowed to deteriorate by successive owners, it finally was acquired and restored by a Canadian snowmobile enthusiast Alain Benoit of Quebec.

Another view of the Honda Raider prototype

A restored Raider snowmobile prototype

Meanwhile Greg, who collects twin track snowmobiles, was able to locate the machine in Canada and negotiate a purchase from Alain. The ownership transfer was completed when Alain delivered the Raider to Greg at the snowmobile museum in Upper Michigan. Greg's interest and knowledge of Raider sleds can be seen in a website he created called "Twin Track World." He calls it "the official website for Raider, Manta and Trail Roamer Snowmobiles."

Honda had also worked with the Leisure Vehicles company to develop prototypes of larger Raider-style snowmobiles, and while that work was underway it was reported that Honda attempted to buy or partner with the Michigan company. However it was said Honda apparently became unhappy with management and business practices of Leisure Vehicles and terminated the business relationship.

Next American Honda sent one of their sales representatives to Troy with instructions to retrieve all their products remaining at Leisure Vehicles. Included in the reclaimed inventory were two prototype snowmobiles which were then taken to a Michigan cycle dealer. The reclaimed sleds eventually were sold by the dealer to customers and through the years they again were sold to other owners.

One of the unusual snowmobiles was painted blue after it started to show signs of age. The other finally was acquired and restored by a snowmobile enthusiast in Minneapolis. Each owner was located and contacted by a Raider collector Kris Wood of Beloit, who was able to purchase each rare prototype to add to his collection of over 150 Raiders. Kris discovered an identification number painted on the side of one of the sleds. The number 4H02 he believed indicated the sled as being 4-cycle Honda #2.

A Honda Motosled prototype

1997 Honda Motosled snowmobile

The relationship with Leisure Vehicles would not be Honda's final venture into snow. In fact during the years that followed Honda was considering new ideas for a snow vehicle which they believed could be appropriate for snow country dealers.

It would take more than two decades before Honda would provide a look at another possible entry into the world of snowmobiling. In 1997 Honda unveiled to selected members of snowmobile publications a prototype called Motosled, which was said to be one of two new concept snow vehicles being tested in North America.

The Motosled actually looked more like a stand-up style personal watercraft. It had a large single ski in front and a 12 x 94 inch track. It weighed in at about 300 pounds and was powered by a 246cc two stroke single cylinder engine. The snowmobile was steered by a movable handle bar which included a thumb type throttle. Other features included electric start, CDI ignition and oil injection.

A writer for Snow Goer Magazine was invited to view and test ride Honda's latest snowmobile concept. He reported his ride on the Motosled as enjoyable, but also learned a rider could tire out sooner because of the energy and skills required to operate the machine while in a standing upright position. He also observed the sled seemed to be made for deep powdered snow or on a frozen lake, but could be a "boring ride" on well groomed trails.

The Motosled may have met Honda's desire to be innovative, but also may not have displayed profit potential for U.S. Honda dealers and consequently did not end up on their showroom floors. However the unique machine was reported to remain available in Japan. Honda was also said to be developing an all electric snowmobile.

1993 Honda EZ-Snow

MAKE IT GO... IN THE SNOW

Honda took another adventure into snow travel in 1993 when the company created the "Honda EZ-Snow," apparently intended to be a companion to the Honda Cub EZ-90 cycle which was sold in the U.S. from 1991 to 1996. The cycle was targeted for beginners with a 90 cc two stroke engine and automatic transmission.

The EZ-Snow was a snow conversion kit with a ski in front and a small track attached under the rear. About 250-300 kits were made but apparently none were officially offered in the U.S. and those that were produced were marketed only in Japan.

Maine Forest & Logging Museum

CHAPTER 14

IT WAS BIG and IT WAS FIRST

The 15 ton Lombard Log Hauler was the first successful use of continuous track to provide snow vehicle propulsion. Alvin Orlando Lombard patented his giant steam powered vehicle, affectionately called "Mary Ann," in 1901.

Lombard was raised on the farm and forest lands of Springfield, Maine. As a youth he was mechanically inclined and worked with sawmills in the Maine woodlands. In the 1890's he moved to Waterville, Maine where he invented wood barkers and chip machines for the pulp and paper industry.

His inspiration to build a log hauling machine came after a chance encounter on a train ride with a prosperous lumberman E.J. Lawrence who complained about the hundreds of draft horses his company had to use to perform needed work in the woods. Lawrence asked Lombard if he would create a machine to haul logs, and the talented blacksmith accepted the challenge. He designed and worked on the idea until just over a year that he was able to fire up his first prototype machine. He applied for a patent for the "logging machine" on November 9, 1900 and his patent was granted May 21, 1901.

Lombard continued to make his log hauler and was able to hold a successful demonstration which produced orders for his new invention. With orders in hand he established the "Lombard Traction Engine Company" in 1904 to begin production in Waterville, Maine.

The first Lombard haulers burned wood with an upright locomotive type boiler which powered two engines. Operating the machine required a four-man crew comprised of engineer, fireman, conductor and steerer. The steerer often was viewed as the crew's hero as he sat in an open area in the front of the hauler dealing with flying sparks from the boiler stack, which often set his clothing on fire while he turned the large steering wheel to avoid trees. The steering wheel controlled two large skis beneath his platform. Sometimes a machine owner would build a cab over the steering area to help protect the steerer from the sparks. The Lombard machine could simply be defined as a multi-ton snowmobile with a top speed of 5 mph.

IT WAS BIG and IT WAS FIRST 127

Maine Forest & Logging Museum

The first log haulers would pull three loaded timber sleds, but later models usually would pull up to eight sleds with 100,000 board feet of logs. One record-setting train was said to have pulled 24 sleds and had a total length of 1,650 feet.

Detroit Public Library

"Hemlock Special," Cheboygan, Michigan

Lombard's Factory

Lombard built 83 of the steam powered haulers until he began building 6-cylinder gas powered units in 1917 and then changed to diesel power in 1934. The fuel-powered log haulers were redesigned with a front truck-like appearance, and it was said they were less powerful than the earlier steam powered haulers.

In 1904 Charles Tolles of the Phoenix Company in Eau Claire, Wisconsin learned of Lombard's new machine. He made a trip to Maine where he bought one and also acquired the rights to manufacture them. The Phoenix Company had been started by Tolles' father in 1861 to manufacture sawmill machinery and logging equipment. However after obtaining the rights for the log hauler, the company produced 200 Phoenix Log Haulers in the next nineteen years, and for every machine produced in Eau Claire Lombard was paid a royalty fee of $1,000.

Phoenix Log Haulers in production in Eau Claire, WI

The Phoenix machines had 100 horsepower four-cylinder engines operating at 200 pounds of steam per square inch. They could burn wood or coal with one and one-half tons of coal required for ten hours of use. Water for the boiler was needed every four or five miles. To obtain water a hose was attached and the pressure from the engine would draw water from sources along the way such as creeks or lakes. When water would be hard to find a full tank sleigh also was pulled by the Phoenix.

The Phoenix log hauler attracted attention from timber companies in Canada where at least six machines were sold. The first was purchased in 1905 by the Sturgeon Lake Lumber Company where it was used to haul lumber from its mill to Prince Albert about thirty miles away. A letter to the Phoenix Company in 1909 from the lumber company expressed great satisfaction with the machine's performance.

The letter read "our engine has worked steadily this winter all day and sometimes into the night in a temperature varying from 30 below to 55 below. There are some

Phoenix ready for shipment to Finland

heavy grades upon the road which the engine climbs well. The train consists of seven loaded sleighs, a large water tank and a heavy caboose for the crews. We consider the engine is doing the work of 40 four-horse teams."

The Pas Lumber Company of Manitoba had several Phoenix engines, and one Phoenix shipped to Canada was a 1910 model used in the Yukon Territory.

In 1913 the first of two engines to be shipped to Finland was for an order placed by Richard Hugo Sandberg who was forestry manager for Kemi Paper Company. He ordered his second Phoenix a year later and the engines became known as "Sandberg Locomotives." The machines have been preserved at two museums in Finland.

The Phoenix company continued to make improvements to their log hauler and in 1920, like Lombard, converted to internal combustion engines. However at the same time large logging operations in the area started to decline and finally stopped a few years later. The Phoenix Company ceased manufacturing log haulers in 1923.

In Maine, the last Lombard engine was built in 1934 because the old log hauler was being replaced by heavy duty trucks and caterpillar type vehicles. The company produced a line of diesel tractors until 1936, and after Alvin Lombard died in 1937 it provided construction equipment and process machinery for the pulp and paper industry until 1954.

The Lombard steam log hauler was designated a national "Historic Mechanical Engineering Landmark" by the American Society of Mechanical Engineers, and a plaque was erected in 1982 at the Lumberman's Museum in Patten, Maine.

A larger tribute to Lombard exists in the snow and ice covered Antarctica where "Mount Lombard" was selected by the place-names committee to "recognize the American Engineer for creating the earliest successful over snow tractor." Mount Lombard is the highest peak in a mountain range in the southern section of the icy continent.

Lombard log haulers have been preserved at four locations in Maine, including the Forest and Logging museum in Bradley where a 1910 model was completely restored to operating condition. The restoration project was done at the museum with assistance from the staff and students from the University of Maine Engineering Department. The extensive restoration began in the 1990's and included needed construction of many components. The work finally was completed in 2014 with the Lombard then being pressed into action by the museum for demonstrations and rides during special events.

Volunteers involved in a 20-year Lombard restoration

Old Phoenix engines can be viewed at a few Wisconsin locations including the logging museum in Rhinelander. Another one has been restored to operational condition and can be viewed at a logging museum about 50 miles east of Rhinelander in Wabeno, Wisconsin. It is one of three which were used in that area by the G. W. Jones Lumber Company until 1929.

Phoenix steam engine at Rhinelander logging museum

Phoenix being used by G.W. Jones Lumber

The old and abandoned engine was acquired in 1935 by the township for $200 when assets of the former logging company were being sold and plans were being discussed to build a logging museum in Wabeno. The museum opened four years later and the Phoenix with a sled of logs was proudly placed in an adjacent outside display. The production number on the Wabeno engine is #79.

The process to restore the engine to operational condition began several years later when two local business men, Frank Sinard and Milt Lang became interested in that possibility. Previously they had restored a rare Case Steam Traction engine which they were showing at steam machine gatherings throughout the state.

In 1963 Sinard and Lang requested and received permission to restore the Wabeno Phoenix to operating condition. With the knowledge gained from their previous restoration experience the two men worked for more than two years, often having to fabricate missing parts in their shop. In July of 1966 the restoration of the Phoenix was completed and the engine was fired up.

Although the Phoenix had finally become fully operational it was only driven twice a year from its museum exhibit to be featured in the town's annual logging festival and again in the "Wabeno Steam Up Days," which is an annual celebration of historical technology put on by the Antique Power Association.

Wabeno Logging Museum

Wabeno Logging Museum

Paul Ehlinger operating the Phoenix at the Wabeno Museum

The Wabeno steam hauler is maintained by a committee of local men who are interested in preserving the Phoenix and its unique history. Paul Ehlinger is a member of the group who enjoys explaining to visitors the details and history of the amazing machine. Paul also has been selected as one of the drivers when the engine is moved from its museum site, something which began to happen more frequently starting in 2016.

Originally the Phoenix only was to be used for local events, but as news of its operational ability spread other events began requesting its participation, and the town board reversed an earlier no-traveling decision and agreed to share their unique piece of logging history. Paul Ehlinger then assumed the responsibility of scheduling and arranging transportation for the engine and serving as a Phoenix driver at events throughout Wisconsin and Upper Michigan. One of the most meaningful journeys was when the Phoenix was returned to its "birth place" in Eau Claire to participate in a city centennial celebration.

Paul Ehlinger adding wood to the Phoenix boiler

Paul Ehlinger with the scale model at the Logging Museum in Eau Claire

A visit to Eau Claire's Paul Bunyan logging museum also provides an opportunity to view an operating 1/6 scale model of the Phoenix. Master model builder Dan Kiekhafer traveled to Wabeno to take exact measurements before making his own patterns and castings. The completed model is on a special elevated skid with rollers to allow viewing of the moving tracks when the model is running.

Boston Public Library

CHAPTER 15

Snowmobiles on Antarctica

Thirty-nine years after Lombard invented his giant log hauler, another unbelievably large snowmobile was built as part of an ill-fated project which was endorsed by the U.S. Government. The idea was to create the perfect snow vehicle to be used for expanded exploration on the ice covered continent of Antarctica. Previous attempts at using early snowmobiles there had resulted in only limited success. The new idea would be a colossal vehicle but instead it became a colossal failure.

Dr. Poulter with proposed Snow Cruiser design

The greatly over-sized snowmobile was to be built for the planned third expedition by famed Antarctic explorer Admiral Richard Byrd. Called the "Snow Cruiser" it was designed by Dr. Thomas C. Poulter who had served as second in command on Byrd's previous second expedition. Poulter's inspiration to build the Snow Cruiser came from an incident on that previous trip when Admiral Byrd nearly lost his life. Byrd had become isolated by severe weather at a distant base camp and several rescue attempts were made before he finally was rescued.

The snowmobiles used for the rescue attempts were Ford and Snowbird halftrack adaptions which could move through the snow but were not able to cross the numerous large crevasses, and they also faced the problem of moisture freezing in the fuel lines. Dr. Poulter then realized the need for a vehicle which would specifically be designed for Antarctic conditions.

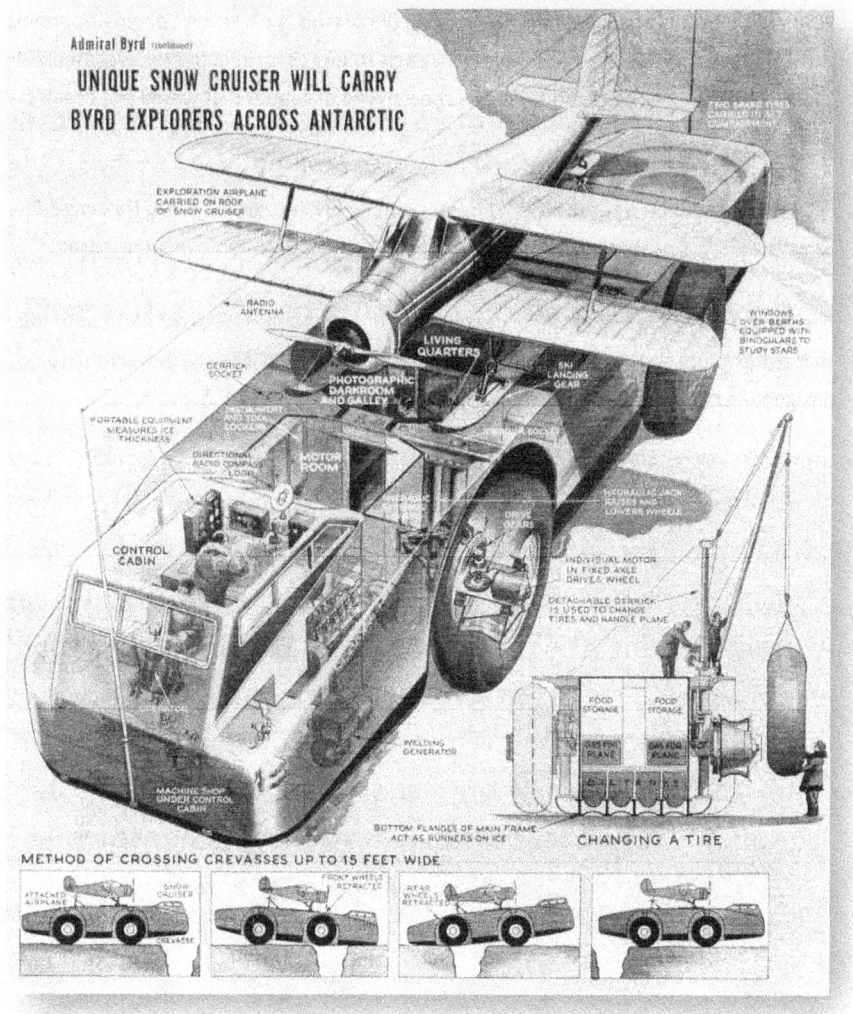

When he returned to the United States Poulter became the scientific director for the Research Foundation at the Armour Institute of Technology in Chicago where he directed his staff about design ideas for the proposed Snow Cruiser. Two years later the final design work was presented to Byrd Expedition officials who provided $150,000 to allow construction to begin. The expeditions had attracted generous financial backers including Edsel Ford, John D. Rockefeller, Jr. and the National Geographic Society. The construction got underway at the Pullman Company in Chicago and was completed in October 1939.

MAKE IT GO... IN THE SNOW

The finished product was a behemoth, unlike any snowmobile built before or since. It was 56 feet long, 20 feet wide and 16 feet high. It weighed more than 30 tons when fully loaded with a years supply of provisions for a four man crew and needed diesel and aviation fuel. The aviation fuel would be used for a reconnaissance aircraft which was carried on the roof and fitted with skis. The Snow Cruiser was powered by two diesel engines. It had four-wheel steering and was equipped with hydraulic wheel jacks to be used when crossing wide crevasses.

The front wheels were to be retracted with the rear wheels pushing the vehicle, then the rear wheels would be raised, and the front wheels lowered to pull the Cruiser over the opening. The tires, ten feet in diameter, were specially manufactured at the Goodyear plant in Akron, Ohio. The Snow Cruiser became known as "Byrd's Snowmobile."

When construction was complete the next challenge was to drive the huge vehicle on public roads from Chicago

A test at the sand dunes

to Boston and to arrive by November 15th when Byrd's ship, the USCGC North Star was scheduled to leave for Antarctica. The cross country journey of 1,020 miles began October 24, 1939 with some testing to be performed along the way.

The Cruiser's top speed was to have been 25 mph, but on a first run only 10 mph was reached before the pace finally increased to 20 mph. An off-road test of climbing was done near Gary, Indiana on a 19 foot high sand dune. It took seven tries for the vehicle to finally go over the top, after six of the large tires had failed. New spare tires were later picked up during a stop at Goodyear in Akron.

Along the way there were mechanical repairs to be made, and the vehicle's huge size added to the problems when the Cruiser became stuck on a bridge, later collided with a truck, and finally careened down a hill and into a 10-foot deep stream. In addition travel was slowed when crowds of spectators jammed the streets to witness the unusual vehicle traveling through their towns.

MAKE IT GO... IN THE SNOW

Richard Byrd's giant snowmobile aboard the North Star in Boston on November 14, 1939

The Snow Cruiser finally limped up to Byrd's waiting ship at Boston's Army Wharf just three days before scheduled departure. President Franklin D. Roosevelt had become interested in Byrd's third expedition and on November 25, 1939 endorsed the venture as a government sponsored trip. The growing war talk in Europe had caused the President to see the need to establish two permanent basis in Antarctica.

The ship with Snow Cruiser and crew arrived at Little America in the Bay of Whales, Antarctica in early January 1940. After unloading the giant snowmobile the crew discovered that the large treadless tires provided little forward travel as they spun freely sinking into as much as three feet of snow. They also learned the best traction was accomplished when the vehicle was driven backwards. Consequently the Snow Cruiser's longest antarctic trip was 92 miles all driven in reverse.

The large treadless tires provided little forward travel

The planned snowmobile trip to the South Pole never took place, and the large snow vehicle was parked in a shelter made of snow blocks and canvas to occasionally be used as sleeping quarters by some of the men. The crew continued to work with Admiral Byrd conducting experiments and ice core sampling.

Additional federal funding for the expedition was canceled and the country's attention became focused on World War II. Dr. Poulter returned to the United States on January 24, 1940 still with the belief that his Snow Cruiser could eventually solve the problems of snow travel on Antarctica.

An international expedition in 1958 used a bulldozer to uncover the abandoned Snow Cruiser which was covered by 23 feet of snow. Inside they found it as the crew had left it with papers, magazines and other scattered items. They were unable to completely uncover or retrieve the vehicle.

Boston Public Library

The abandoned Snow Cruiser was covered by 23 feet of snow

Later expeditions found no trace of the Snow Cruiser and due to the changing motion of the ice shelf, it probably was carried out to sea and is at the bottom of the Southern Ocean.

Byrd's third expedition with the Snow Cruiser undoubtably was the most elaborate attempt to achieve successful powered snow transportation in Antarctica. But other ideas were tried earlier in the history of the snow covered continent.

One determined individual who was the first to drive a car on Antarctica also returned two years later with a second idea. It was 1907 when Bernard C. Day was working at the Arrol-Johnston car company in Paisley, Scotland. It may have been his mechanical ability or maybe just his availability which caused him to become a member of Sir Ernest Shackleton's British Imperial Antarctica Expedition aboard the ship Nimrod. An Arrol-Johnston car had been donated for the expedition by William Beardmore, a major sponsor of the planned adventure who also had recently taken control of the Scottish car company to save it from bankruptcy.

Some thought the donation was an attempt to gain publicity for the car. However, the Arrol-Johnston Company was recognized as the world's first to produce an off-road vehicle. In addition the 4 cylinder 15 horsepower engine was alcohol-fueled and air-cooled, and the car had special increased traction tires.

Bernard Day would drive the car and serve as the mechanic as one of the expedition's goals was to reach the South Pole. Sir Shackleton thought they might be able to travel 150 miles in 24 hours to achieve a successful sprint to the pole.

However it was not to be as the engine had not been tested in extreme cold weather and a suitable system to improve traction had not been devised. When first taken off the Nimrod and placed in loose snow the car's wheels

Arrol Johnston car before taken to Antarctica

turned rapidly burying themselves in deep snow and preventing any forward movement.

The car was hoisted back on the ship and written off as a means for any extended snow transportation. However the car eventually was used again but with only moderate success on hard packed smooth surfaces. It was of help in establishing two supply depots 10 and 15 miles from the base camp and Day calculated the total distance the car traveled during the expedition at about 500 miles while being able to carry loads of up to 1800 pounds.

When the expedition concluded the car was shipped to New Zealand and then back to England where it was displayed in the English Museum.

Bernard Day was selected for his second adventure on Antarctica in 1910 when he was named a motor engineer for Robert Falcon Scott's expedition on board the ship Terra Nova. Day was the world's only engineer with any experience in operating vehicles in Antarctica and having learned about the problems of wheeled cars during his first trip he took with him three tracked vehicles. They simply were basic machines with an engine mounted between two driven axles.

Towing sleds with car. 1908

Antarctica's first tracked snowmobile

One of the three was lost through sea ice during the unloading. However the other two proved to be useful in hauling supplies when conditions were suitable. Day was constantly repairing them because of the challenges of

Day's make-shift garage of packing crates

operating in the antarctic environment. They would overheat and continue to sustain mechanical and structural damage until Day was no longer able to repair them and finally they were abandoned.

With his mechanical service no longer needed Day returned home in 1911. He received England's Polar Medal for his participation in two expeditions and for his pioneering work with powered snow vehicles in Antarctica.

Since those first attempts for snow transportation on Antarctica there have been many others who were successful as snowmobile technology improved. The continent of Antarctica is not owned by any country, the result of a treaty signed in 1961 by over 50 nations declaring it a site for scientific interest and having freedom for research. Current snow travel involves more than 70 research stations, but only about one half of them are occupied year round.

A recent successful expedition in 1958 included a world famous adventurer best known for his mountain climbing achievements. Sir Edmond Hillary became the first person to reach the South Pole using a track type powered vehicle. The feat also made his team the first to reach the pole since 1912 when Robert Falcon Scott had arrived there by dog sled.

Just five years before his South Pole trip Hillary had been part of a British team to reach the summit of Mt. Everest and become the first men to stand on the "roof of the world."

To reach the South Pole Hillary was a member of a New Zealand research team which was part of a larger British antarctic expedition led by Vivian Fuchs who also hoped to be first to reach the pole. During the summer of 1957-58 Hillary's four man team had left the food and fuel depots

Edmund Hillary on his converted Massey-Ferguson tractor

to be used by the Fuchs team. But apparently Hillary became tired of waiting for Fuchs and used his snow-tracked Massey Ferguson tractors for what became his famous and controversial "dash to the pole." Hillary was known for his "devil-may-care" attitude and his team charged forward over snow ridges, deep soft snow and dangerous crevasses to reach the pole on January 4, 1958, sixteen days ahead of Fuchs.

His achievement was acknowledged and praised but at first it appeared to some to be an arrogant maneuver as it was against instructions from the committee coordinating the expedition. However it was revealed that Hillary and Fuchs previously discussed the idea and no objection was raised at the time for each team to make the attempt.

1969 Sears Hillary Snowmobile

Hillary seemed surprised when he learned after his team's trip that the committee had not granted them permission. His later autobiography was titled "Nothing Venture, Nothing Win."

Ten years after Sir Edmund left his mark at the South Pole he received another snowmobile honor when Sears began selling a snowmobile named after Edmund Hillary. The sled was built to spec for Sears by OMC and had parts in common with the Evinrude and Johnson snowmobiles of that time.

It was powered by a 28 hp 399 cc Kohler Engine. Features included electric start, battery charged by running engine, and a 20 inch wide cleated track. Sears sold the Hillary sled 1969-1971.

CHAPTER 16

Trail Blazing Pioneers

By the mid 1960's the new and growing popularity of recreational snowmobiling clearly indicated there soon would be the need for snowmobile trails and use areas. There were some who questioned the idea of developing long distance trails or trail systems.

However one group of Michigan snowmobilers set out with their own sleds to prove those doubters wrong, and during the next seven years they traveled over five thousand miles across a dozen states and in two other countries.

154 MAKE IT GO... IN THE SNOW

Frieberg gets the snowmobiles lined up for the start of their first cross country run

These pioneering snowmobilers were known as the "Peninsula Pathfinders" who were based out of Marquette in Michigan's Upper Peninsula. Their leader was "Trail Boss" Ray Frieberg who explained the group's purpose was to promote "snowmobile touring" as a popular winter activity for the near future.

The Pathfinders first long distance ride in 1968 was across the entire upper Michigan peninsula. It was a 498 mile, four day venture from Ironwood in the west to Sault Ste Marie in the east where a winter carnival was being held.

Eleven men riding their own snowmobiles completed the trip. Some manufacturers after learning of the plan, offered to provide snowmobiles and other equipment. But the offers were refused as the goal was to make the trip an example of what would be a typical non-commercial event promoting only the future for long distance cross-country snowmobiling.

After four days and 498 miles, they arrive in Sault Ste Marie.

Each day's journey covered more than 100 miles and often local snowmobilers would meet the Pathfinders to serve as temporary trail guides in their areas. Snowmobilers from St. Ignace escorted the group for the final miles into Sault Ste Marie where they received special recognition at the winter festival.

Trail boss Ray Frieberg reported only minor repair problems were experienced during the entire trip which did not cause any changes to their original four day schedule. The Pathfinders believed the trip had charted a trail of nearly 500 miles which would be important in years to come for other snowmobilers as well as organizations in planning future trail needs.

The Pathfinders second cross country trip was a more ambitious plan to travel 350 miles in only two days. To add to the challenge the difficult trip began at the northern tip of Upper Michigan's Keweenaw Peninsula, an area often recognized for receiving some of the nation's heaviest annual snows with accumulated depths of 300 inches or more.

The hardy snowmobilers started their trip in the small community of Copper Harbor on Saturday morning February 15 and it would be completed very late Sunday night in Green Bay, Wisconsin.

The plan for the first day was for the 16 riders to travel almost 200 miles to Iron Mountain, Michigan located near the northern border of Wisconsin. That destination ultimately was reached but their travel schedule was seriously delayed. Having to push through snow often as deep as six feet during the first leg of the trip resulted in frequent stops for repairs and the exhausted snowmobilers didn't reach their planned over night rest stop until 4:00 am Sunday.

With less than four hours rest and a quick breakfast the riders began the second day's journey over hills and rough terrain of northern Wisconsin. One sled was seriously damaged and had to be replaced after the driver crashed at high speed into a large snow covered boulder.

Snowmobile damaged during trip

The Pathfinders made a planned stop about 60 miles north of Green Bay at the Wisconsin town of Crivitz where a snowmobile event was being held. The state's Lt. Governor Jack Olson was included in a local group of snowmobilers who met and escorted the Pathfinders for 15 miles to become honored guests at the event.

The final segment of the two day trip brought needed trail-guide assistance from Green Bay's Packer City snowmobile club, and the long and often difficult adventure finally was completed at 11:45 pm in the parking lot of the Packer's Lambeau Field. A nearby restaurant had remained open to provide meals for the tired and hungry Upper Michigan snowmobilers. Their total elapsed time on their long ride was estimated at forty hours.

The third annual cross country ride for the Pathfinders achieved added significance as they became one of the first snowmobile groups to cross Michigan's famous Mackinac Bridge, which connects the Upper Peninsula to lower Michigan.

The snowmobilers left Marquette Thursday evening February 12, 1970 for what was supposed to be an easy two-day 140 mile ride to St. Ignace where the bridge crossing would begin. From there it would be another 260 miles to their ultimate destination of Cadillac in lower Michigan.

However the trip's first miles were anything but easy as the 13 snowmobilers faced 20 below zero temperatures and battled strong blowing snows which buried the trail and caused carburetor freezing problems and spark plug fouling.

A plaque showing route from Copper Harbor to Green Bay was presented to Ray Frieberg by the Packer City Snowmobile Club

The tired and cold Pathfinders finally reached St. Ignace at 9:30 Friday evening and early the next morning had to attach wheels to the sled's skis to accommodate a requirement for the bridge crossing.

A state police escort led the riders safely across the bridge to Mackinac City where the ski wheels were removed and the weather and travel conditions had improved. It then was another 85 miles to Saturday night's rest stop at 7:00pm in Grayling, Michigan.

The group set out for their destination Sunday morning and along the way was able to enjoy an extended travel break to be welcomed guests at an annual ice fishing event at Houghton Lake. Later as they drew closer to Cadillac they were joined by growing groups of local snowmobilers who had learned about the historic ride. The Peninsula Pathfinders arrived at their destination at 5:30 pm after a four day trip of 394 miles, traveling first through cold blowing snowstorms but ending at times on scenic guided trails and frozen lakes.

Pathfinders crossing the big Mackinac Bridge

When the Pathfinders planned their fourth annual cross country adventure, it was apparent that both the quality of the snowmobiles and the trails were improving. Consequently the distance to be traveled was expanded to 475 miles and the travel time was reduced to three days instead of the previous four day trips.

The group of ten riders left Marquette headed for Brainerd, Minnesota on February 3, 1971 and during that first day, in spite of deep snow covered trails they were able to travel 122 miles to Bergland in far western Upper Michigan.

An easier run the second day allowed the the snowmobilers to travel 175 miles to Solon Springs in northwest Wisconsin. For the third day the group traveled through Minnesota where they encountered sub zero temperatures and winds gusting up to 50 miles per hour. They were cold and tired but were able to reach their Brainerd destination in time for a late evening meal.

Only minor mechanical problems were experienced during the three day run, and the Pathfinders decided they would observe their successful trip with a winter campout a few weeks later.

It may have been the recent memories of another successful trip, or possibly the campfire conversation which inspired the Pathfinders to begin plans for one of the longest cross country excursions to be taken by a club. It would turn out to be a trip of 1700 miles traveling through seven states in fourteen days.

The fifth annual trip made by nine club members began January 22, 1972 near Marquette, Michigan and reached its destination February 5th at Yellowstone National Park in northwest Montana.

The venture was well organized and planned with each snowmobiler carrying with him items such as parts, tools and extra fuel. A bus had been converted to accommodate ten people, and it would meet the group each evening at a prearranged location. In case of an emergency such as being snowed in and unable to reach the bus, each rider also carried a survival kit including rations, matches, candles, a first aid kit and a sleeping bag.

Problems along the way included days of severe weather with high winds and extreme cold temperatures. Twice there also was unexpected difficulty caused by a lack of snow. The first time was a fifty mile stretch near Devils Lake, North Dakota, and the second time it was 137 snowless miles between Lewiston and Gardner, Montana. In those two situations the sleds were loaded onto a trailer which was towed by the bus.

However the group also received welcome assistance, including warm meals provided by snowmobile clubs along the way, and by local law enforcement officers who provided safe escorts through their communities.

Trail boss Ray Frieberg summarized the adventure by explaining that the trip created many new experiences, and he added "as far as I am concerned every day was worth it."

The trailblazing group recorded their average daily travel distance of 123 miles.

After accomplishing what some had feared would be an impossible snowmobile trip to northwest Montana, the Pathfinders were seeking their next travel destination which would provide even greater challenges from a different terrain and riding conditions.

They apparently found what they wanted for their 6th annual cross country trip because they selected a new eastbound route taking them through Ontario, Canada before returning to the U.S. to conclude the adventure at the Atlantic Ocean.

The dozen experienced trail riders began their 1200 mile expedition January 19, 1973 from Harvey, Michigan in the Upper Peninsula. They entered Canada at Sault Ste. Marie and traveled 860 miles through Ontario with stops in Bancroft and Prescott and through the Algonquin Provincial Park to Perth. The club re-entered the the states at Ogdensberg, New York and set their sites for Portland, Maine.

Like their previous trip to Yellowstone the Pathfinders again had the back-up support of their converted bus, but this trip provided more opportunities for evening motel accommodations.

Pathfinder makes history with Atlantic Ocean ride

The riders crossed Vermont's Green Mountains and the White Mountains of New Hampshire. They visited Lake Placid, New York and entered into Maine during a snowstorm at Fryeburg. On January 30 the Pathfinders were welcomed to Portland where they received the symbolic "key to the city."

They traveled on to Old Orchard and at 2:30pm on January 31 were near their destination where TV and press reporters had gathered to witness the Peninsula Pathfinders jump their sleds over a snowbank and drive into the cold water of the Atlantic Ocean!

Most of those who participated in the historic snowmobile "ocean dash" came out soaked as a cold and wet souvenir of their experience.

No serious mechanical problems were experienced during the trip, but there was a lack of snow in two areas causing the sleds to be hauled for short distances. Trail boss Ray Frieberg observed that the club's annual extended mile trips were also serving to prove snowmobiles had become capable of making safe long distance trips.

The seventh and last written record of a long distance trip by the Peninsula Pathfinders turned out to be their most exciting after they decided to carry the club's flag to a second foreign country.

It is easy to understand why they selected Finland to be their destination because Michigan's Upper Peninsula is well known for its Finish history and traditions.

Considerable preparation and planning was needed to accomplish the unique adventure which began March 21, 1974 by auto from Ishpeming to Lansing and the next day again by car to Detroit Metro Airport. Their international flight carried the twelve snowmobilers to Helsinki and then the following day they were flown to what became their snowmobile base of operation at Rovaniemi. There "Winha" Snowmobiles and a guide were provided by Polar-Metal-Plast, at that time the only snowmobile manufacturer in Finland.

The first trip in Finland took the Pathfinders across the Arctic Circle where they paused to plant an American flag and hold a brief ceremony with Lake Superior water they had brought for the event.

Another trip took club members near the Russian border, and during their time exploring Finland they also learned new trail cooking methods and enjoyed meals including reindeer steak and fresh salmon. They also observed that Finland terrain was similar to Upper Michigan with many lakes and rivers and forests of pine and white birch.

To mark their final night in Rovaniemi the Pathfinders were honored at a hotel dinner attended by more than 400 people including representatives from area news organizations, local officials and special guests from Norway and Lapland.

Finally returning home by air and auto, Michigan's famous traveling snowmobilers arrived back in Ishpeming the evening of March 31. They brought with them treasured memories of an amazing adventure which covered over 13,000 miles, including 670 kilometers by snowmobile in Finland.

CHAPTER 17

Homemade Snowmobiles

Through the years the challenge of powered over-the-snow transportation has attracted the creative spirit of thousands of inventors. Some of their ideas provided the foundation for future successful products or even businesses. Other ideas simply solved a snow travel problem being experienced by the inventor. Some ideas never evolved beyond the talking stage and remain waiting to be created.

This portion of the book offers a tribute to those homemade snowmobile inventors while presenting a small sampling of their unique and varied ideas.

A photo of one of the earliest of those efforts shows the results of a snowmobile built in England in 1909 by O. C. Johnson. His invention was ten feet long and was powered by a crude track system powered by a "one lunger" engine. It was controlled by a front mounted steering pole which also had a lantern attached, apparently for planned night time travel.

The inventor wanted to share his success so he brought along his wife and their two dogs for a test run. It was reported the machine would travel "on top of the snow... when it worked."

Another homemade idea for snow travel called a "Snow-mo-cycle" was built in 1914 in Jackson, Minnesota. Brothers Frank and Howard Sawyer created their unusual machine which provided side-by-side seating for their winter travels. The seating was positioned over a rear motorcycle

wheel which was powered by a four cylinder Henderson cycle engine mounted at the very front of the Snow-cycle's long wooden frame. Steering was accomplished with a long steel rod connected to the front skis and extended back to a steering wheel in the passenger seat.

A more recently built homemade snowmobile received unexpected recognition when it was put to use at an official Michigan rocket launching site in 1967. Located on the snowy northern tip of the Keweenaw Peninsula the rocket range had been established by the University of Michigan's Institute of Science and Technology to provide a location for launching research rockets into Lake Superior.

University of Michigan

Elmer Isaacson who lived in Mohawk, Michigan, not far from the rocket site enjoyed working with new ideas in his small shop at home and had decided to build his own snowmobile. After Elmer had completed his unique yellow sled he became an interested observer and then a participant in the Arcas launch program of 1967.

University of Michigan

The slender Arcas rocket was six feet long and weighed 76 pounds with a payload of meteorological instruments. The rockets were launched to an altitude of 41 miles before plunging into Lake Superior 20 miles east of the launch site.

Isaacson used his new yellow snowmobile to transport the rockets out to the launch site. His snow transportation was important during the winter months of the research

University of Michigan

because snows on the Keweenaw often reach depths of eight to ten feet or more. The rocket range project was shut down in 1971, but the yellow snowmobile continued to be enjoyed by the Isaacson family for many years.

Decades before Michigan's rocket project the annual deep snows on the Keweenaw Peninsula resulted in creating many ideas for powered snow travel, and one of those inventions became a life saver. A Calumet auto dealer in 1927 was developing his idea which would convert one of his cars for use in deep snow. Paul Pawler modified a Chrysler Overland model with a track-type system covering the four rear wheels, along with a set of skis mounted to replace the front wheels.

Pawler's idea proved successful when he was able to drive through forty miles of deep drifted snow to provide aid for badly injured crewmen who had been rescued from a Lake Superior shipwreck east of Copper Harbor. In the winter the tiny northern community was isolated because their one small access road remained unplowed.

Pawler's snow vehicle

Keweenaw Historical Society

Pawler's first snowmobile trip to Copper Harbor transported a doctor for the crewmen who had been provided shelter in a family home. Next Pawler used his invention to bring the most seriously injured men back to the hospital in Calumet-Laurium. On return trips more injured crewmen were taken to the hospital by the snowmobile while others were transported by sleigh. The converted snow auto was credited with helping to save the lives of many shipmates.

Another winter event from the snowy Keweenaw Peninsula serves as an example of how young inventors throughout snow country also became fascinated with the idea of building their own snowmobiles. This story reveals the creative efforts of three high school boys in Calumet, Michigan.

The Krainatz single passenger air sled

Twin brothers George and Lewis Krainatz and older brother John constructed their snowmobile using salvage material. An old V-twin cycle engine was used to power a wooden propeller which the young inventors had hand-crafted in their high school shop.

The loud and strange looking single passenger air sled was being operated on the town's streets until one night when a test run was cut short by a local police officer. After a quick study of the unusual invention he declared "I don't know what that thing is, but get it off the road." Things weren't always easy for those young snowmobile inventors.

Another homemade wind powered snowmobile was the first of three to be built in the late 1920's by Henry Englehart and his son on their farm near Iron River, Michigan. Henry's motivation to create his snow vehicle was the 13-mile unplowed road to town, often covered by drifts up to 10-feet deep.

Iron County Historical Museum

He used a motorcycle engine and attached the hood and seat to a wood frame. Henry also hand crafted the propeller and two long wooden skis. He used that first experience to later build two more air-sleds, but for those machines he used airplane engines for power. His inventions were offered for sale, but apparently were never sold, possibly because of difficult financial times caused by the crash of 1929.

A snowmobile, which was tiny and did not even look like a snowmobile was built in 1936 and was designed for just one specific use. It was the unique creation of Fred Westendorf, a machinist at Wicks Machinery in Saginaw, Michigan. Fred also was an avid ice fisherman and the main purpose for his little sled was to take him fishing on the frozen Saginaw River. The unusual little snow machine had several one-of-a-kind features including retractable foot pegs which made it possible to load the sled into Fred's model A Ford. Power was provided by a 1.5 hp Briggs & Stratton engine which Fred had modified for a little additional power. A spring loaded rear drive wheel was connected to the engine, and when pressure was applied to the front pegs, the wheel would be lowered to make contact with the surface below.

Two wide skis were attached to the rear and a single ski was positioned in front for steering.

When Fred no longer had use for his creation it was placed for sale at an equipment auction where it was viewed with a curious interest by Harold Boyse of Clio, Michigan. Harold had experienced little buying success at the auction that day and made a last minute decision to buy the

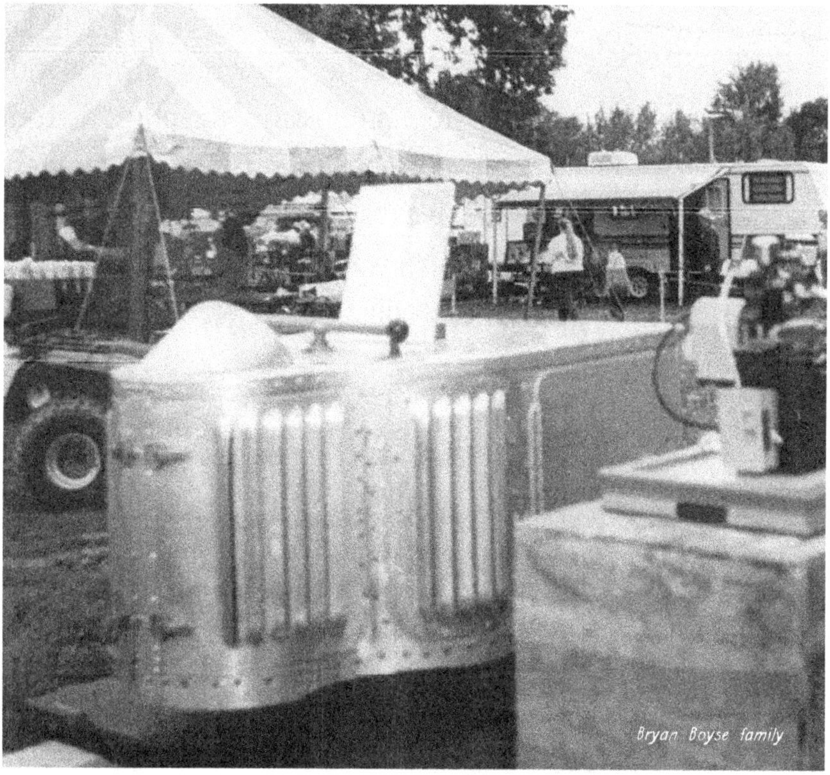
Bryan Boyse family

strange machine while not even knowing exactly what it would be used for, although the sled had acquired the nickname of "Pizza Oven."

Harold finally gave his "antique oddity" to his son Dan Boyse who succeeded in riding the sled in the snow before plac-

Boyse family photo

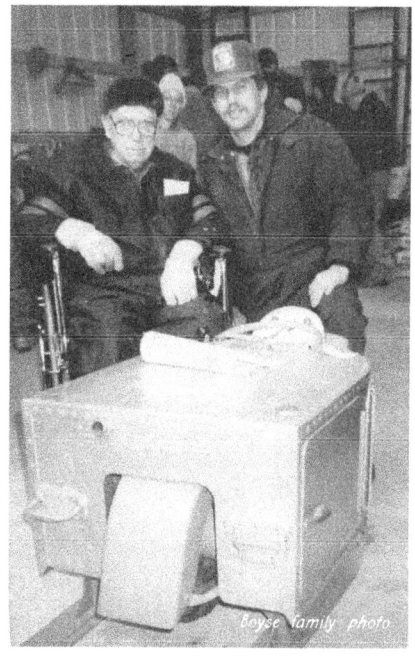

Harold with his son after making the purchase

ing it on display at the Top Of The Lake Snowmobile Museum in Naubinway. Museum visitors are able to get a close-up view because the tiny sled can be inspected while located on top of a table.

The "pizza oven" is the smallest homemade snowmobile at the museum which has a total collection of more than 200 snowmobiles and includes some additional rare homemade sleds.

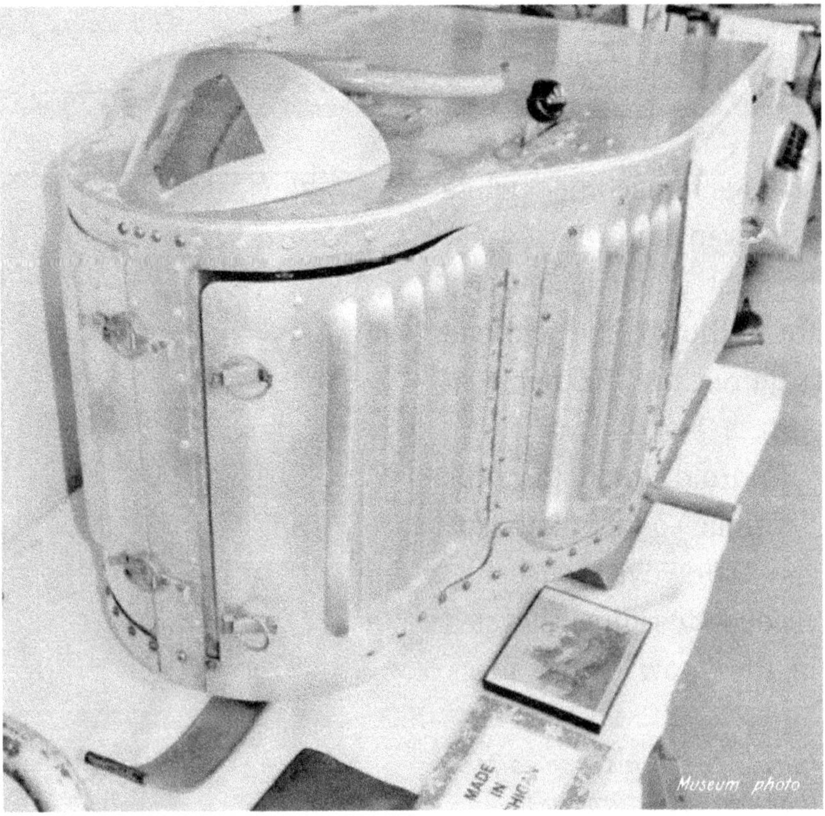

One of them is a snowmobile which was pieced together in 1966 by Ken Rintala an ironworker who lived in Houghton, Michigan. The machine's track is based on an old conveyor belt assembly with metal cleats. Power is provided by a 1958 Briggs & Stratton 14-hp engine using a Salsbury clutch and drive belt. The steering wheel came from a 1950s Plymouth Belvedere.

Also on display at the museum is one of six snowmobiles built in the 50's and 60's by Charles Anderson and his son Melvin of Manistique, Michigan. After looking at a snowmobile in a Popular Science magazine they decided to build their first one in 1957.

Anderson snowmobile at work-in the woods

family photo

On display is their invention of 1963. Anderson was a machinist for a company in Gulliver and built a transmission for his snowmobile which included high, low, reverse and neutral positions. The Andersons would harvest fallen trees in the winter and used their inventions to haul the logs.

A twin track snowmobile built in 1967 is a one-of-a-kind sled which also has been placed on display at the museum. Built by Ken Stanaback of Grand Rapids, Michigan the machine has no skis and is steered by by dual clutches and brakes on the drive axle. Powered by a 400cc Lloyd engine the Stanaback sled has no brakes and is capable of turning 180 degrees in its own length.

These are just a few of the "vintage treasures" to be seen at the museum in Upper Michigan, which was started in 2007 by a group of vintage snowmobilers. The museum is a non-profit organization headed by a board of directors with board chairman Charley Valliers and his wife Marilyn handling the daily operation as well as planning a variety of annual events and activities.

Top of the Lake Snowmobile Museum

CHAPTER 18

Snowmobile Museums

The growing interest in vintage snowmobile racing, trail rides, shows and related activities can be considered as one important reason for the increasing interest in the history of snowmobiles. That interest has resulted in the need to archive, preserve and display snowmobile history. The solution has been the creation of dozens of snowmobile museums throughout the North American snow belt.

Some of the first museums were developed in the early snowmobile states such as Michigan, Wisconsin, Maine and New Hampshire. Throughout this book there are several references to the Top Of The Lake Museum in Michigan's Upper Peninsula. Organized by a group of dedicated snowmobilers, the museum has grown to become one of North America's greatest archives for old and rare snowmobile history and memorabilia.

There are many other museums in snow country and what follows is a random listing of better known museums, including some which were created to feature a special time or activity in snowmobile history.

Wisconsin is home for three popular museums. The Snowmobile Hall of Fame and Museum in St. Germain is dedicated to preserving and honoring the history of those who have been involved in snowmobiling. Each year the museum inducts four new members into the hall of fame. Other museum events include the annual "Ride With The Champs" a classic sled round-up, and the regular vintage snowmobile displays and swap meets.

The World Snowmobile Headquarters Museum is located in Eagle River, Wisconsin on the same site as the famous World Championship Derby track. The museum is dedicated to providing a showcase to preserve and honor the people and machines that have created and maintain the sport of snowmobiling. There are photos and memorabilia representing 59 years of racing. An extensive exhibit by the Antique Snowmobile Club of America includes machines from the early 1950's to modern day models. The museum and derby track are located just north of Eagle River along

U.S. highway 45, and the museum is open Monday through Saturday, 10am until 4pm.

The Vilas County Historical Museum is also considered an important Wisconsin snowmobile museum because it is located in Sayner which has been proclaimed as "The Birthplace of the Snowmobile." The motor toboggan was created there by Carl Eliason in 1924, and the museum is located about a block away from Eliason's original workshop. Eliason's original snowmobile is included in the museum's snowmobile exhibit area along with additional Eliason power toboggans and a collection of other antique snowmobiles and memorabilia.

New Hampshire is home for two established museums, each representing a different time in the state's snowmobile history. The New Hampshire Snowmobile Museum Association was founded in 1985 in Allentown to become the only state operated snowmobile museum in the United States.

It began when the state Parks and Recreation Division provided the needed space in two former CCC (Civilian Conservation Corps) buildings near Bear Brook State Park. That public-private partnership resulted in the creation of a popular one-of-a-kind museum complex to display over 80 snowmobiles and a large collection of memorabilia.

Also in New Hampshire, Crane's Snowmobile Museum was founded in 2004 in Lancaster by Paul Crane a snowmobile pioneer and local legend in the area. At the age of twenty Paul was working for a company in Lancaster which in 1959 became the first Bombardier dealer in the United States. Paul's claim to fame is that he became the first U.S. resident to test drive that new snowmobile at that time called a "Ski

Dog" before the name was changed to "Ski-Doo."

Paul started collecting snowmobiles in 1961 saying he "just didn't want to let them go." Consequently he built his museum to display over 120 snowmobiles, with a couple dozen more awaiting restoration in his shop. He also is reported to be the first antique snowmobile collector in New Hampshire. Paul and his family operate the museum located at 172 Main Street in Lancaster.

In Polson, Montana "The Miracle of America" is not just a snowmobile museum, but the large museum complex does feature the state's largest collection of antique snow vehicles which were built to either cope with or have fun on ice and snow. Included are vintage snowmobiles, snow planes, snow tractors, powered toboggans, snow bikes and other rare snow machines.

The museum's huge collection of historical artifacts are displayed in 42 buildings and in open air exhibits throughout the 4.5 acre site. Founded in 1981 by Gil and Joanne Mangels the one-of-a-kind facility is dedicated to the preservation of one of the largest collections of American history.

A surprising "family built" snowmobile museum is located in a rural area in central Minnesota. Scott Gottschalk didn't realize that his family's intense interest in collecting and restoring antique machines would result in the creation of a snowmobile museum containing over 200 sleds including some rare prototypes and one-of-a-kind models.

It all began when Scott's sons Trevor and Travis began a ten year endeavor to restore old John Deere tractors. Their completed machines received championship awards and special recognition from the John Deere Corporation.

However after restoring sixty tractors the tractor display area was running out of space, and the family decided to concentrate on collecting something smaller. The faded memory of an old family snowmobile was all it took to start the search for antique snowmobiles and build a museum to display them. Scott was pleasantly surprised by many new friends with antique sleds who came forward with ideas and helpful suggestions.

The new museum grew to contain one of the largest collection of air sleds, unusual rare antique machines and vintage racing sleds including Evel Knieval's only snowmobile which was used for a national TV stunt in 1977.

Scott said the family believes in "being care-takers of special pieces of history to share with others." The Gottschalk snowmobile and tractor museums are located south of Kimball, Minnesota and every year attract hundreds of visitors from throughout the United States.

A snowmobile club museum was built in 1985 in Maine after the idea was proposed by a club member of the Northern Trail Cruisers in Millinocket. Steve Campbell first thought about the need for a museum in 1982 after he had located and restored a 1961 Polaris Ranger, and he also reflected on the snowmobile history in Millinocket. His dad Earlan Campbell was Maine's first snowmobile dealer, and from 1961 to 1966 Polaris tested machines in the area because snow conditions and terrain in Maine were vastly different from that in Polaris's home state of Minnesota.

The members of the Northern Trail Cruisers agreed with Steve's idea and organized fund raising events to begin a three-year building project in 1985. The completed museum contains fifty sleds and memorabilia including photos, helmets and snowmobile suits. Many of the sleds have been restored and all are owned by individuals. The museum building is owned and operated by the club and is open weekends during sledding season, as well as for special events including community antique and vintage shows and swap meets. The museum is located at 3 Northern Cruisers Trail in Millinocket.

In Canada it has been called "the most professionally run snowmobile museum in North America. "The Museum of Ingenuity, The J. Armand Bombardier Museum" began in 1968 and opened to the public in 1971. Included is an extensive exhibit about Bombardier which features the history of his snow vehicles and other inventions along with the history of the Bombardier Corporation.

Seventy-five unusual vehicles are displayed including thirty-five carefully selected snowmobiles and not limited to Ski-Doos. The elaborate displays show the development of the modern sport sled and the worldwide snowmobile industry.

Located in Valcourt, Quebec the Bombardier museum is open daily May first to Labor Day, and Tuesday through Sunday the rest of the year.

YOU DON'T NEED TO SAY GOOD BYE...

*To memories made by that exciting
first time snowmobile experience.*

*To the friendships made
while sharing snowmobile adventures.*

*And maybe to the thrill of the challenge
of snowmobile competition.*

*As the modern snowmobile
continues to change and grow in popularity,
don't say good bye to those special memories...*

VISIT A SNOWMOBILE MUSEUM!

About the Author

The author first became addicted to the sport and business of snowmobiling after buying his first sled, an Arctic Cat, in 1967. He purchased that Cat from the first Arctic Cat dealer in Green Bay, a local shoe repair shop which had a total available inventory of two machines.

Jorgensen was fortunate to become a riding member of the pioneer cross country snowmobile group, the Peninsula Pathfinders of Upper Michigan. He participated in the club's first three long-distance rides, including the 1970 trip across the giant Mackinac Bridge which connects lower Michigan to the Upper Peninsula. Although he owned the Arctic Cat, he had been convinced to ride an Eskimo snowmobile and it may have been the only time an Eskimo sled crossed the Big Mac.

He was a news reporter for a TV station in Green Bay, and in 1969 he and a fellow station employee named John

Ireland produced the first consumer snowmobile exposition at the Brown County Arena. In the years which followed, the two snowmobilers produced additional expositions in Fargo, North Dakota; Duluth, Minnesota; Milwaukee, Wisconsin; Chicago, Illinois; Des Moines, Iowa; and Lansing, Michigan.

Jorgensen was one of three snowmobilers who participated in the 1970 Allsport Alaskan Expedition. It was an endurance test for the new Allsport Tracker snowmobile which went from Fairbanks to Seattle, Washington.

The Pabst Brewing Company of Milwaukee contracted with Jorgensen to help introduce Pabst to the new world of snowmobiling. He worked with the brewer to create programs for recreational and snowmobile racing. He organized and participated on the original Pabst Racing Team, which raced Polaris and Ski-Doo sleds. The team also raced for three years on the Winnipeg to St. Paul cross-country event, and during one of those years Jorgensen drove a new John Deere LC.

Jorgensen served on the board of directors for the United States Snowmobile Association Central Division, including one year as President. He also was President of his local snowmobile club in Green Bay.

He published a monthly snowmobile magazine *Midwest Sno-Trails* for six years and also wrote a weekly snowmobile column for United Press International.

In looking back at over a decade of snowmobiling, it might best be summarized by his oldest daughter...when as a first grade student she was asked what does your father do? The answer: "He snowmobiles."

www.ingramcontent.com/pod-product-compliance
Lightning Source LLC
Chambersburg PA
CBHW070537170426
43200CB00011B/2452